Witches
and Warlocks
of New York

Witches and Warlocks of New York

Legends, Victims, and Sinister Spellcasters

LISA LaMONICA

Globe
Pequot

ESSEX, CONNECTICUT

Globe
Pequot

An imprint of Globe Pequot, the trade division of
The Rowman & Littlefield Publishing Group, Inc.
4501 Forbes Blvd., Ste. 200
Lanham, MD 20706
www.rowman.com

Distributed by NATIONAL BOOK NETWORK

British Library Cataloguing in Publication Information available

Library of Congress Cataloging-in-Publication Data Available

ISBN 978-1-4930-6341-3 (paper: alk. paper)
ISBN 978-1-4930-6342-0 (electronic)

♾ ™ The paper used in this publication meets the minimum requirements of American National Standard for Information Sciences—Permanence of Paper for Printed Library Materials, ANSI/NISO Z39.48-1992.

This book is dedicated to Joe Netherworld, whom I wish I had met on the journey of writing this book. He was truly a special person, and I thank Angella Valentine, his sister, for sharing so much with me after her loss. This book is dedicated also to my niece Nikki, who died in childbirth in April 2021 while I was working on this book. May she rest in peace.

The Witch's Daughter **by Frederick Stuart Church** Library of Congress, Frederick S. (Frederick Stuart) Church, 1842–1924, artist and founding member of the Art Students League of New York

Contents

Introduction

What did witchcraft mean to the men and women accused of it by the neighbors and judges who condemned them?

Three centuries of "burning times," witchcraft hysteria ran from the fifteenth century, peaking around the year 1600, to the eighteenth century. The horror may have ended, but the practice of witchcraft and the fear of even the word has not.

Fortunately, our justice system has evolved since those times.

A world authority on the subject of witchcraft resided for a time right here in New York State. From England, Rossell Hope Robbins is sadly no longer with us. It would have been fascinating to interview him for this book. He was for a time a University of Albany professor before his passing at his home in Saugerties in 1990. Robbins explained that "witchcraft is not anthropology, folklore, mythology or legend." Satanism or sorcery it is not either.

Writing a book is a journey, involving meeting many new people and research in many locations. In writing this book, one of my closest friends gave me Rossell Hope Robbins's book *The Encyclopedia of Witchcraft and Demonology.* I only wish I could have started this book while he was still with us here in New York, and long for the opportunity to have met him.

Cornell University, Ithaca, New York, houses the first known book written on the subject of witchcraft from 1497. It was previously owned by a monastery of St. Maximin at Trèves; and subsequently three hundred people were sentenced to death as a result of the book. George Lincoln Burr, Cornell University president Andrew D. White's personal secretary and librarian, later acquired it on one of his many book-buying trips throughout Europe.

Ironically, I started writing this book in my house on Church Street in Nassau, upstate New York, on a street surrounded by churches. It amused me at the time, but also made me think about how churches at certain times in history may have been terrifying to many accused of witchcraft.

Fortunately, we do not live in the burning times anymore.

Halloween, 2020

Nassau, New York

History and Origins of Witchcraft

The word *witchcraft* is fascinating to some, ugly to others, and terrifying to many.

Witchcraft is a word that cries out for our attention, whether we like it or not, on behalf of the many poor souls who perished, but also for our understanding of the many who still practice it.

Witches and witchcraft, words having been around for a thousand years, are somewhat benign to most people these days. In olden times, though, it must have been terrifying to be left-handed—for then you could be labeled a witch by your neighbors, and put to death. Strange how witches and witchcraft evoke fear in people who may not understand the truly heartbreaking things that were done *to them*.

Justice was at the mercy of superstition, and trials in those days were not designed to prove innocence but rather to condemn the accused as fast as possible. We all know that superstition and gossip were enough to be charged; torture was then used to get a confession. It is truly heartbreaking to think of the thousands of people, including young children, who died horrible, unnecessary deaths at the hands of their accusers.

Description de l'assemblee des sorciers qu'on appelle sabbat. *Histoire des imaginations extravagantes de Monsieur Oufle;* Division of Rare and Manuscript Collections, Cornell University Library

Germany, Switzerland, and the UK had many villages wiped out or completely taken over with "thousands and thousands of the stakes to burn the witches," wrote an all-too-experienced witch judge in 1600. Here in rural parts of America, just being an older woman living alone such as a widow could be enough to be accused as a witch. The Hudson Valley's Hulda the Witch is a prime example of one such woman being misunderstood.

You could be considered a witch or warlock (male witch) if you had a wart, bunion, or scar. You could be accused of being a witch if you were a gypsy. We know that witches were burned at the stake, but why?

To the religious and superstitious, witches, warlocks, and witchcraft were considered treason against God. "Roasting and cooking them over a slow fire is not really very much," said Jean Bodin, who was a French lawyer, "and not as bad as . . . the eternal agonies which are prepared for them in hell. For the fire here cannot be much more than an hour or so before the witch dies."

An accused witch or warlock had to disprove rumor and gossip and prove their innocence—in most cases, an impossible task. It's important to realize that no accused was ever found to be innocent.

Well, except Westchester's Katherine Harrison in 1670. A servant in the earlier part of her life, she was later left substantial wealth upon her husband's death and within two years became the subject of rumored witchcraft. Her case would become notable in creating a different legal response to the subject of witchcraft in America.

But before that, while the hysteria was still in England, it's not hard to understand why some wished to leave this world once accused. One woman in 1662 said to the Lord Advocate "under secrecy that she had not confessed because she was guilty, but being a poor creature who wrought for her meat, and being defamed as a witch, she knew she would starve for no person thereafter would either give her meat or lodgings, and that all men would beat her, and hound dogs at her, and that therefore she desired to be out of the world."

And if the accusation of being a witch yourself wasn't bad enough, there was the idea that your pets or "familiars" especially if black—black cats, black dogs, black bats—were the Devil's gift to you to carry out evil in exchange for your allegiance to him.

By the seventeenth century witchcraft had become big business, with many people profiting from the deaths of the accused. Occupations such as court official, judge, torturer, carpenter building firestakes, and guard all flourished. If the accused and killed person owned anything, it was surely confiscated as well.

We know from George Lincoln Burr's research that this happened to Westchester's Katherine Harrison:

A warrant to the Constable of Westchestr to take an Account of the Goods of Katherine Harrison.

These are to require you to take an Account of such Goods as have lately beene brought from out of his Ma'ties Colony of Conecticott unto Katherine Harrison, and having taken a Note of the perticulers that you retorne the Same unto me for the doeing whereof this shall be yor warrant. Given undr my hand at Fort James in New Yorke this 25th day of August 1670.

The most severe forms of torture were used to get the accused to accuse others, thereby keeping the killings going and the money flowing. It wasn't just poor common peasants that were accused and died; it was people of noble birth as well.

It was also about control. Control by the Catholic Church over the population. Control of women by men. Control over the less fortunate by the ruling class. Control over who made money in business.

Female sorcerer unleashes a storm with her upturned cauldron, 1555. Public domain image, woodcut; Division of Rare and Manuscript Collections, Cornell University Library

In contrast to Massachusetts and other states, New York had significantly less witch trials due to the large Dutch influence in the state's early history. It's not that the Dutch were without superstition, they just did not believe in witch hunting and killing, and took a much more logical approach to justice in these matters. According to George Lincoln Burr,

> It is not strange that in the Dutch colony of New Netherland we hear nothing of witches. The home land of the Dutch had, beyond all others, outgrown the panic. . . . No wonder, then, that (as Mrs. Van Rensselaer tells us) "the one and only sign of the delusion . . . to be found in the annals of the Dutch province is a fear expressed by Governor Kieft that the Indian medicine-men were directing their incantations

against himself." Accusations of witchcraft the New York jurisdiction did not wholly escape; but they followed the English occupation and were, in differing ways, a legacy from New England. Even the Dutch dominion had included towns peopled from New England; and it was to these that in 1662 (the same year in which, as we have seen, he was interceding with the Connecticut government for his young kinswoman Judith Varlet) Governor Stuyvesant found it wise, while granting them their own magistrates and their own courts, to prescribe that "in dark and dubious matters, especially in witchcrafts, the party aggrieved might appeal to the Governor and Council."

While the hysteria in Salem, Massachusetts, regarding witches was full-blown, New York had only two well-known cases and became a sanctuary for accused witches to flee to from other states if they could. What helped New York avoid the witch hysteria was the strong and increasing Dutch influence: Dutch leaders actually opposed witch hunting. Witchcraft accusations in New York received a bit more skepticism by the state's justice system.

It was not witches who burned. It was women.

—*Fia Forsström*

Halloween/Samhain and the Hudson Valley Origins

When witches go riding,

And black cats are seen,

The moon laughs and whispers,

'Tis near Halloween.

—Anonymous, early 1900s

L ong before blockbuster movies or even radio shows, people devoured and were terrified from reading Washington Irving's "The Legend of Sleepy Hollow," believed to be America's first published ghost story. Before *Twilight*, "Sleepy Hollow" was a paranormal romance tale allowing the Hudson Valley to almost take ownership of Halloween in America. America was hungry for such stories at the time, making Irving a best-selling author here and in England, unprecedented at that time, and he became America's first writer to support himself solely from his craft.

"Sleepy Hollow" incorporated some German and Dutch folklore into its tale. First inhabited by the Mohicans and settled before 1651, Kinderhook, New York, has an intriguing historical past. While the town has ties to the American Revolution and was home to America's eighth president, Martin Van Buren,

Two witches putting a snake and rooster into their cauldron, 1493. *Von den Unholde[n] oder Hexen* by Ulrich Molitor (1470–1501); Division of Rare and Manuscript Collections, Cornell University Library

Kinderhook is best known for being the origin of "The Legend of Sleepy Hollow." The story's main character, Ichabod Crane, was based on Washington Irving's close friend Jesse Merwin, a teacher who moved to Kinderhook in 1808.

Due to the story's success and its terrifying icon, the Headless Horseman, Kinderhook and the Hudson Valley have evolved from farmland and sleepy folklore to an area full of cultural interest. "Kinderhook is noted as one of the more haunted places in the Hudson Valley, which is saying quite a lot for an area inhabited by all manner of ghosts, ghouls and things that go bump in the night. After all, Washington Irving's Headless Horseman rode through the Hudson Valley in pursuit of Ichabod Crane, just to name one of the most famous examples of Hudson Valley folklore," explains Kinderhook author Bruce G. Hallenbeck. In this spooky tale, Irving believed Sleepy Hollow to have been bewitched by a "witchdoctor" who may have been loosely based on local Hulda the Witch.

To the ancient Celts, October 31 was a potent time to commune with spirits, since it fell exactly between the Autumnal Equinox and the Winter Solstice. The Pleiades constellation also was at its highest point in the sky at midnight October 31, making it possible, they believed, for the dead to walk the earth. The veil between the worlds was, on this day, at its thinnest and the souls of the dead returned to visit those they knew in life.

The Celts viewed time in pairs: winter/summer, dark/light, night/day. Cusp moments at times of sunrise and sunset and the nights of a waning or waxing quarter moon were occasions when one time period had not quite ended and another had not begun, thus normal laws of time and space were suspended and time stood still. Past, present, and future could then overlap. The period between October 31 and Yule was considered a time not even existing on the earthly plane. Samhain was summer's end, with November 1 being the Celtic New Year.

A suspension of the laws of time allowed boundaries between present and future to disappear, and barriers between the worlds of the living and the dead were broken.

While summer seems to sing with its greens, its flowers, and its blue sky with big white puffy clouds, fall conveys a dread, a fear to some. Colors are somber after October's blaze of glory. The rustling now-dead leaves sing a different song. Skies can look ominous and foreboding instead of happy. Dead leaves are heard on the ground as in the trees. What was that noise? The trees themselves, now bare, reveal their gestural shapes with a tangle of reaching arms and fingers. Weeping willows in the wild winds sway to and fro, reaching out to passersby. Their movement now gives a different impression. Summer's breezes are now a biting cold wind. The deadness of fall, a mystery to some, is frightening to others.

Halloween, at summer's end (Samhain), was a grieving time because of the sun's decline, but also a thanksgiving (Harvest Home) to the sun for ripening the grains and fruits of summer. After bringing the cattle in, some leisure time would commence after the hard work of summer. Druids, priests of the Celts, made sacrifices of animals and also of war prisoners, often burned alive in wicker images—bonfires on hills meant to appease their gods and guarantee abundance of harvest.

October 31 was the last night of the old year and the start of the new year. With new fires on New Year's Day, black sheep were sacrificed and divination was done from the ashes, and these fires were meant to protect home and hearth for the coming year.

Troy resident, film and TV critic, and author Peg Aloi, wrote for the Witches' Voice/Witchvox and stated, "For early Europeans, this time of year marked the beginning of the cold, lean months to come; the flocks were brought in from the fields to live in sheds until spring. Some were slaughtered and the meat preserved to provide for winter. The last gathering of crops was known as 'Harvest Home,' celebrated with fairs and festivals. Communion with the dead was thought to be the work of witches and sorcerers, although the common folk thought nothing of it. Because the rise of the Church led to growing suspicion of the pagan ways of country dwellers, Samhain also became associated with witches, ghosts and other spooky things." Peg teaches media studies at Albany's College of Saint Rose, is a practicing witch of Celtic/Sicilian heritage, and wrote the foreword to *The New Generation Witches* (2008) and *Lights, Camera, Witchcraft: A Critical History of Witches in American Film and Television* (2021). One of her students at SUNY New Paltz fondly recalled Peg as "one of my favorite professors at New Paltz. She cares about her students, has a wondrous sense of humor and taste in music/pop culture. You will learn a ton from Aloi. If you have to take Media and Society, take it with Aloi, you will not regret it."

The following poem by longtime editor of the *New York Evening Post* William Cullen Bryant, written in New York City, beautifully describes summer's end:

The Death of the Flowers

The melancholy days are come, the saddest of the year,
Of wailing winds, and naked woods, and meadows brown and sere.

Heaped in the hollows of the grove, the autumn leaves lie dead;

They rustle to the eddying gust, and to the rabbit's tread.

The robin and the wren are flown, and from the shrubs the jay,

And from the wood-top calls the crow through all the gloomy day.

Where are the flowers, the fair young flowers, that lately sprang and stood

In brighter light and softer airs, a beauteous sisterhood?

Alas! they all are in their graves, the gentle race of flowers

Are lying in their lowly beds, with the fair and good of ours.

The rain is falling where they lie, but the cold November rain

Calls not from out the gloomy earth the lovely ones again.

The wind-flower and the violet, they perished long ago,

And the brier-rose and the orchids died amid the summer glow;

But on the hills the golden-rod, and the aster in the wood,

And the yellow sun-flower by the brook in autumn beauty stood,

Till fell the frost from the clear cold heaven, as falls the plague on men

And the brightness of their smile was gone, from upland, glade, and glen.

Immigrants brought their legends with them to America. Ireland's history of Samhain was written between the seventh and twelfth centuries; their beliefs about witches at Halloween came with them to America.

It was believed that one of the dates witches gathered was October 31: Samhain, Halloween, the Day of the Dead, All Hallows' Eve. Then, it was believed, witches would travel by broom and convene with the Devil, cast spells, and cause misfortune to the mere mortals around them. They wrote their names in his book and were carried off to revelry on this night. New witches were pricked with a needle by him as their initiation into the coven. On Halloween night, the Devil was worshipped and sometimes appeared as a goat, while witches were accompanied by owls, bats, and cats; frantic dancing was done and considered to be wicked.

Halloween party invite. Courtesy of John Schobel

By 1986, Wicca was recognized as a religion here in America, and it became protected under the Civil Rights Act of 1964, which prohibits discrimination based on religion. In 2018, *Newsweek* estimated that there were one and a half million practicing witches throughout America.

In American Colonial times, Halloween wasn't celebrated much at all, but these days it's a $7 billion a year industry. Halloween parties have always incorporated apples, nuts, doughnuts, cider, and popcorn in celebration of harvest gatherings. Halloween is still an important holiday for modern witches, who take this time to honor lost loved ones and practice divination using tarot and runes. It is a time to invite lost loved ones to visit, not through summoning and séances but through meditating, visualizing, and also by astral projection for those with that talent. Troy-based Peg Aloi stated in personal correspondence to me, "Thanks to many news media articles in recent years, many people now understand that Samhain is a festival celebrated by modern witches and that there is an overlap with Hallowe'en." Halloween, Peg says, is also "about immersing ourselves for a few days in a mode of revelry that allows us to confront something many of us fear deeply—death."

In September 2016, Peg learned from her friend Jo Frost that her father Gavin Frost had passed. Gavin, with his wife Yvonne, had founded in 1968 the Church and School of Wicca, helped author over two dozen books on magic and witchcraft, and also gave workshops at Sirius Rising, festivals held in upstate New York at the Brushwood Folklore Center.

In the 1960s and 1970s, in addition to the vandalism taking place on Halloween night, many movies were made pertaining to the occult, causing fear and suspicion of pagan-based practices. A lot has changed since that time. Whereas in the 1990s we'd see Halloween television commercials and decorations only in the days leading up to Halloween, today we are saturated with Halloween and witch images year-round. These days it's easier than ever to connect with Facebook and Instagram groups devoted to witches, Samhain, and Halloween. In the 1990s there was scant media coverage on witchcraft, but it is everywhere on social media and popular on television shows, and there are many magazines now totally devoted to the Craft. Every fall major clothing designers are inspired by witch-type wardrobes and come out with a line of seemingly "witchy" fashions for Fashion Week.

An article in the *Christian Work: Illustrated Family Newspaper* from 1894 described how new Halloween was to us at that time. The author stated: "Now that our maturing nation is awakening more and more to the value of holidays, there springs into recognition and observance some peculiar 'days' which have only recently been specially noted. There are those of us whose hair is merely sprinkled with gray who in childhood only heard of All Saints Day and Halloween as a vague mention. But lo! Today our blithesome sons and precious young people count among the festive occasions of the golden Autumn the Halloween party. And we are glad of it." The writer further states that "Halloween was superstitiously regarded especially by the Scottish peasantry as a time when witches and evil spirits went back and forth on dark mysterious midnight revels."

HONORING THE EARTH: THE WHEEL OF THE YEAR

Time is considered by many to be linear, though it may actually be circular and folding onto itself.

The wheel of the year is cyclical, with many sabbats and festivals that mark time, marking a significance to practicing witches. Sabbats also have correspondences and edible flowers associated with them. Predating Christianity, the events were later borrowed by Christians, and all represent honoring the earth and its cycles.

Yule occurs on the Winter Solstice, December 21, which is the shortest day and longest night of the year. Christmastime festivities ramp up and we look forward to the days getting longer. Rosemary resembles our Christmas trees in form and heavy pine scent, and is wonderful to cook with atop of roasts like turkey, chicken, and duck. Folklore tells us that people used to plant rosemary near doors, as it was believed that a witch couldn't enter a dwelling unless she could count all of the rosemary's leaves.

Imbolc begins February 2, marking the midway point of winter. People look forward to longer days, and toasted pumpkin seeds are a tasty treat during this time by the fire. It's a time to honor the fertility of the land and clearing away of the past. The pumpkin is a bit of a rarity due to its flowers, leaves, seeds, and pulp all being edible. Nothing goes to waste.

Ostara and March 21 represent the first day of spring, with the egg and the hare being symbols of fertility and the abundance of the universe. It's easy to see why Easter came from Ostara. Also an equinox, days and nights are of equal time. We start to see a bit more color including lavender, a beautiful purple flower used fresh or dried in teas and on top of pastries and cakes.

Beltane is celebrated April 30 to May 1, and now the earth smells and looks like spring. Now is the time to use the rose hips gathered in the fall, steamed in hot water with rosemary to clear up and hydrate skin, which often takes a beating from winter's cold outside air and dry indoor heat. Beltane represents fertility, love, and sexuality.

Litha, June 21, is the longest day of the year, with plenty of light returning to us. Cornflowers appear everywhere with their light blue color and are used in teas and salads and atop cakes. Litha is when we start to see some results of seeds planted earlier in the year.

Lammas, August 1 and 2, takes us to the midway mark between summer and fall. Marigolds, also known as calendula, are plentiful; you see them everywhere. Used for medicinal purposes such as burns and rashes, marigolds are also edible and commonly used in salads, scrambled eggs, and quiche.

This time of year also starts to mark harvesting.

Mabon is from September 21 to 24, when the aster star-shaped flowers reign. Also an equinox, day and night are of equal time on the 21st, so balance, symmetry, and harvest are themes here. Used in teas, as garnish, and atop cakes, asters were also used by Native Americans for digestive purposes. Flowers are consumed cooked or raw.

Samhain and later Halloween, which derived from this fall harvest festival, starts on October 31 and lasts through November 1. The veil between the living and the dead is at its thinnest at this time, and bonfires mark the final harvest being brought in, including pumpkins. While we now mainly turn them into jack-o'-lanterns for Halloween, the pumpkin offered many sustaining foods—leaves, flowers, seeds, and pulp—for our ancestors.

HALLOWEEN NOW AND THEN

In October 2021, Elizabeth Stack, executive director of the Irish American Heritage Museum (the only one of its kind in the United States), located at 21 Quackenbush Square, Albany, was featured on WMHT's weekly arts show *AHA! A House for the Arts*. Elizabeth detailed the Irish influence on what we now know as modern-day Halloween, based on the Celtic fall festival of Samhain, the harvest season celebration of bringing in the last fruits and nuts of the season.

Dressing up in ancient Ireland was to protect oneself from evil spirits roaming about. The Irish folk religion was strong and carried over with them to America upon settling here. The Irish custom of carving turnips was based on the Irish folktale of Stingy Jack, Jack the Lantern. With pumpkins being so large and plentiful in America, turnips were not carved here, but rather the big orange orbs that we have come to love during the Halloween season.

"Imagine what people thought when they picked up the *New York Times* on October 31, 1969, and read that Dr. Raymond Buckland and his wife, Rosemary, were meeting that very night with their coven in a Brentwood, Long Island basement. Nude. That their neighbors—clerks, a barber, housewives—were with them, hopping around the basement on broomsticks, and that they regularly practiced magic in coven gatherings around each full moon." Friend and fellow Halloween-lover Lesley Pratt Bannatyne wrote this in an essay on how Halloween celebrations changed in the twentieth century. "In America, there's only one group of people who believe that the spirit world emerges at Halloween. Witches," Lesley says.

From her essay I learned of Raymond Buckland having created the Buckland Museum of Witchcraft and Magick in 1966 in his Long Island home, the first of its kind in America. Buckland had visited the late Gerald Gardner on the Isle of Man, and inspired by Gardner's collection, decided to start collecting similar artifacts in New York. From 1966 to 1973 Buckland displayed occult artifacts, including artifacts from the Salem witch trials, that he had acquired from all over the world. His career with British Airways provided him with many enviable travel opportunities.

Buckley's collection included his artifacts as well as those from Gerald Gardner, Aiden Breac, Lady Rowan, Aleister Crowley, Sybil Leek, Anton LaVey, Israel Regardie, Christopher Penczak, Stewart Farrar, Janet Farrar, and Scott Cunningham, and from leaders within the pagan community.

Due to the uniqueness of this one-of-a-kind museum, the world's press took notice. The *New York Times, New York Post, Newsday, Look Magazine, Cosmopolitan, Esquire,* and many other publications featured stories, and the Metropolitan Museum of Art in New York asked to display some of Buckland's artifacts. Buckland was then busy with radio and television appearances as well as writing assignments for a long time to come. As he moved to other states, the museum went with him and now resides in Ohio since 2015.

The museum's website, bucklandmuseum.org, features its YouTube channel with fascinating videos that include interviews with Raymond Buckland on witchcraft.

Witches Raymond Buckland and Scott Cunningham were interviewed together on Halloween 1986 on *Twin Cities Live* before a live television audience who, along with callers, had the opportunity to ask both witches questions on witchcraft. First, the men made clear that witchcraft predates Christianity by at least a thousand years and witches now and back then have never believed in Satan, nor do they worship him. Buckland gave a few examples of the types of witches such as Saxon, Celtic, and Druidic. Witchcraft's One Rule was defined: "An you harm none, do what thou will."

Both men also explained a little of the Rule of Three: Whether doing good or bad deeds, the results return to you threefold. They pointed out that a difference between witchcraft and many religions is that witches and Wiccans do not aggressively push their belief systems on others in ways that a number of religions are known to do.

The television host asked the men, "What is Halloween and what does it mean to a witch?" Buckland explained its ancient Celtic origins going back possibly twenty thousand years as a fire festival celebrating a change of seasons, honoring the dead, and speaking to those who have crossed over during this time of the thinning veil between this world and the world of the dead. Halloween, he said, is to witches what Christmas is to Christians. An audience member asked about the pentagram and whether or not it was a symbol of evil. Buckland explained that it is not; it symbolizes life itself and witches use it as their symbol.

Buckland and Cunningham were asked, "What powers do witches have?" It was explained that many witches have the ability to bend time, have clairvoyant or psychic abilities, and can direct energy to change outcomes (magick). Of course, the audience and television host were hungry for examples, and Buckland did not disappoint when he told the story of an elderly neighbor who had serious problems with other neighbors and wished that he could move but had no means to do so. Buckland and his coven did some magick—chants and manifesting—to try to help this man. A week later, the elderly man's circumstances changed dramatically for the better when his uncle unexpectedly died, leaving him a small fortune that allowed him to move fifty miles away, buy another house, and have no neighbors.

Some might call it a coincidence, some synchronicity, and others chance. But these are the types of changed circumstances that witches seek to bring about from their magick.

These days Halloween generates around $7 billion annually in sales of all things Halloween. Millions of people gather to watch the New York City Village Halloween Parade, which, with close to sixty thousand costumed parade marchers, is the nation's largest public Halloween event and also has the distinction of being the nation's only major night parade.

In 2000 the parade was televised for the first time by USA and Sci-Fi networks with Susan Sarandon as the host, and the following year it was a unifying recovery event after the tragedy of 9/11. The parade draws thousands of costumed performers, musicians performing music from all over the world, and artists to create a truly

Participants in the 2019 New York City Village Halloween Parade. Courtesy of Village Halloween Parade, Inc.

unique and inspirational event. It is believed to bring in around $90 million annually to the city, giving some area businesses and restaurants their best night of the year. It's an event with many big corporate sponsors, but the parade always seeks donations and volunteers interested in being part of the festivities. These festivities bring about goodwill and lasting positive memories for tourists visiting the city, sometimes only for this event.

Jeanne Fleming, producer and artistic director, has run the parade annually since 1979 while living at the historic Rokeby estate in upstate New York's Red Hook. The estate has significant historical value, as it was built two hundred years ago on land granted to Colonel Pieter Schuyler by the Crown in 1688 and has remained in the family ever since. The land was used by tenant farmers with Colonel Henry Beekman, Margaret Beekman Livingston, and Alida Livingston as landlords, then later in the 1800s William B. Astor, the son and principal heir of John Jacob Astor, built the main house that is known today. A workshop on the property produces puppets featured in the parade, on land the native Lenni-Lenape tribes of ancient times had planted corn on.

Rokeby estate and its library. Library of Congress

Jeanne was one of the enthusiastic creatives I corresponded with while writing this book, and she generously loaned images and her time, during her busy schedule of planning and fund-raising for the parade. Gratitude goes to her and people like her who keep Halloween alive in modern times in a very big way.

"If the light and the leaves and the weather are right, we're transported back to where we can almost see our friends running around in Zorro capes, or the flick of a monster's tail in the shadows," says Lesley Pratt Bannatyne in her book *Halloween Nation* (2011). Halloween lovers love a parade and everything associated with the holiday. In 2008, when Lesley had interviewed Jeanne, it was mentioned that three hundred purple witches were planning to attend the parade that year. Jeanne was quoted in Lesley's book as saying: "Sometimes I really do believe when I look down at the parade that these are the same people who have always been doing this. They're ancient spirits, just the latest reincarnation of them. They feel familiar to me." And on All Souls' Day 2021, Jeanne wrote to me that: "To me, it is nothing more than the first magic circle—it's just that now more hear the call! The spirits that come are today's version of those original ones . . . hearing the voices of the ancestors."

Another popular Halloween event is the Great Jack O'Lantern Blaze, a magical walk-through experience produced by Historic Hudson Valley at the historic Van Cortlandt Manor where visitors marvel at around seven thousand lit carved pumpkins made into various characters and shapes with synchronized lighting and music. The blaze is the largest and was the first in the nation, having begun in 2005, with a location in Old Bethpage now as well. This event and the celebration of the pumpkin and Halloween holiday demonstrates how the Hudson Valley still honors our ancient ancestors who brought their Samhain/Halloween traditions and folklore here with them.

The first book-length history of Halloween in America was written by Ruth Kelley, a librarian, and published in 1919. *The Book of Hallowe'en* is a must-have for some hard-to-find history of the holiday's origins in other countries and how it took hold in America. "No custom that was once honored at Halloween is out of fashion now," Ruth said in her book. A Halloween costume pageant in Fort Worth, Texas, in 1919 comprised four thousand schoolchildren. But sadly, many school districts have done away with their Halloween class parades. Yahoo Life states: "Halloween festivities may alienate and exclude students and staffers who may not celebrate for various personal or religious reasons as the holiday, with both its pagan roots and connection to All Saints' Day, is seen as too Satanic for some Christians and too Christian for some Muslims and Orthodox Jews." It has also been suggested that it may be a hardship for some students who may not be able to afford costumes. Many schools, in an effort to be more inclusive, have started to celebrate a "Harvest Day" in the fall.

Halloween is a community holiday; it celebrates the change of seasons, darkness falls earlier, and we turn more to hearth and home. Halloween celebrates being accepted for however you present yourself, and you're allowed to be strange at this time. It is a celebration of fall's colors and creativity. It's a time to imagine and fashion yourself as something else, with witch costumes being one of the top choices for children and adults alike. Like Lesley said in her book, even in modern times witches creep us out and fascinate us at the same time. Witches are, always have been, and may always be mysterious as well as misunderstood. Lesley also pointed out that the witch is "the only feminine holiday icon in a year crowded by men." All of our other holiday icons are males.

In the 1970s, Halloween became a bit of a concern as vandalism rose in terms of people throwing eggs at cars, soaping windows on homes, and stringing endless amounts of bathroom tissue among trees. For a while, it became a time that many adults dreaded and the cleanup after was significant, and that is something I remember in upstate New York while growing up. Fortunately, this trend didn't last or continue to ruin the holiday for the rest of us.

In 2019, a nationwide petition circulated in hopes of changing Halloween to the last Saturday in October, making it more convenient, some parents and teachers argued, since children would not have to get up early the next day for school. The date of this holiday originated in the ancient Celtic celebration of Samhain, and has not been changed because more people than not voiced this concern.

Many children wind up being socialized out of their interest in witches and magic by society. It should remain important to allow children to celebrate Halloween with all of its attendant festivities.

Even in her 1919 book, Ruth Kelley detailed how Americans have embraced Halloween, adopting the customs and festivities that originated overseas in early times, and it is especially true these days. In the early part of the twentieth century, during what has been called the Golden Age of Postcards, Halloween postcards were especially adored. Now collector's items, many were produced with witch imagery, rich colors, and embossing by Valentine & Sons Publishing Co. and by F. A. Owen Co. in Dansville, New York. They were not expensive to buy or send and became a big part of Halloween customs in America.

Witches started to become synonymous with Halloween in America in the 1800s when immigrants like the Irish, who came here due to famine in their country, brought their beliefs with them. But there had long been a connection between witches and Halloween in Europe, going back to the time of the Druids and their Samhain rituals. Almost a million Irish immigrants came to New York in the early to mid 1800s, and they really were the group that had the most impact on Halloween becoming so prominent here in America, and New York's Hudson Valley especially. Pumpkins native to America were huge compared to the turnips the Irish had been using as hollowed-out lanterns in their countryside on autumn nights.

Women who were known as healers became labeled as witches, seen with their brooms that many used to cleanse a space before rituals, and even to hop a creek with. This was associated with flying with them, thus some of our earliest Halloween imagery was created. The Esperance Witch, for example, was accused of being able to "fly" across a river.

Modern witches believe in sharing the bounty of harvest season with others as one of Halloween's features and appreciating the beauty of the autumn season and its colors, which are in such contrast to the colors of summer. Apples, pumpkins, squash, bonfires—all are plentiful during fall. Carved pumpkins after Halloween are then put out for animals to feast on.

The following verse from the Wiccan Rede, a witches' manifesto, beautifully captures this end of summer:

As the old year starts to wane the new begins, it's now Samhain.
When the time for Imbolc shows watch for flowers through the snows.
Harvesting comes to one and all when the Autumn Equinox does fall.
Heed the flower, bush, and tree by the Lady blessed you'll be.

Starr RavenHawk of the Wiccan Family Temple Academy of Pagan Studies in New York City says, "Samhain starts at dusk on the 31st, ending the evening of November 1st. Because Samhain is our High Holy Day, our New Year, we do a grand celebration and dress up—the idea of dressing up is to use your magick to become what we want to be for the coming year. We invoke our future by wearing what we want to create for ourselves, the way we want our community to see us. We are casting a spell about who we are and what we are going to become in the coming year. Most witches dress in their finery, wearing their jewelry and best magickal clothing. Some may do it in a comical, fun way. We may focus within ourselves to look 'through the glass darkly,' developing our divination and psychic skills. It also allow us a greater awareness and connection with the realms of magick and with those who have gone before."

The Upstate Witches and Pagans group chants this on Samhain:

> Hoof & horn, hoof & horn,
> All that dies will be reborn.
> Corn & grain, corn & grain,
> All that dies shall live again.

Spells, Symbols, Sigils, and Superstitions

There's no devil in the craft.

—*Sally,* Practical Magic

SYMBOLS AND SUPERSTITIONS

The Apple Spell:

One I love, Two I love, Three I love I say,

Four I love with all my heart,

Five I cast away.

Six he loves, Seven she loves, Eight they both love,

Nine he comes, Ten he tarries,

Eleven he courts,

Twelve he marries.

—*Spooky Halloween*
Entertainments, 1923

Over the centuries many superstitions have arisen around the subject of witchcraft and the symbols associated with it that linger in people's minds even today. Cats and bats, black pointed hats, brooms and moons, pentacles and pentagrams, and big black cauldrons have long been associated with the witch archetype.

Wikipedia states, "Superstition is the belief in supernatural causality—that one event causes another without any natural process linking the two events—omens, prophesies, etc., that contradicts science; particularly the belief that future events can be foretold by specific (apparently) unrelated prior events, and can be interpreted as 'standing over a thing in amazement or awe.'"

Stirring the Pot, by Hudson, New York–based artist Joseph Holodook. Courtesy of Joseph Holodook

The idea of cats having nine lives goes back to ancient Irish beliefs that a witch could turn herself into a cat and back eight times, but on the ninth time, she would remain permanently as a cat.

The black cat has long been a symbol of a witch's "familiar" or "familiar spirit" and make no mistake—the cat was considered to be a smaller version of a witch's evil intentions or to actually be the Devil himself. It was believed that he could turn himself into a black cat to socialize with his witches. Since the Devil was believed to have made a pact with a witch to do his bidding, the cat was a lower-ranking demon, a domesticated animal, given to her to advise and carry out malice.

Marion Paull in her lovely book *Creating Your Vintage Halloween* (2014) states, "A story that crops up from time to time is that a 13th century pope, Gregory IX, was responsible for linking black cats to Devil worship, leading to their long-term mass extermination and thus, indirectly, a pandemic of the Black Plague." As we know, rats then multiplied like never before, carrying the fleas that carried the disease that wiped out much of Europe at the time.

And what did a witch feed her familiar? Her blood. Therefore any strange markings on her body would have been considered proof of this by the ill-informed and narrow-minded.

Black cats were revered in some cultures like ancient Egypt, but some religions wishing to wipe out other religions labeled black cats as evil, and unfortunately this superstition lasted much longer than it should have.

Black hats, tall and pointy, may originally have been a way for female brewers to stand out in a crowd. Brewing beer was mainly a woman's task up until about the 1500s, at a time when many made beer at home for the rich nutrients and to utilize grains. Women who were alone due to being a widow or not yet married may have excelled at this task and chose to earn money by selling their crafted beer and ales at market.

During the Middle Ages, tall, pointed black hats and cauldrons were a common sight in marketplaces where women were making beer; cats kept rodents away from the grains, and the broom was a store sign letting it be known that beer was for sale. Trouble began when rumors of witchcraft started circulating, perhaps instigated by men wishing to exclude women from this money-making enterprise. It was easy to accuse women of being a witch and casting doubt over what potions they were making in those cauldrons. As men wanted more control over the ale-making business, accusations flew.

Mickie Mueller in her book *Llewellyn's Little Book of Halloween* (2018) states, "When the churches converted the Celts, they called their old traditions of magic and reverence for the earth evil. In the Middle Ages they even portrayed witches in art wearing pointed hats which was the style worn by country women in the last areas to give up Samhain traditions."

Brooms also were thought to be a phallic symbol that was in contrast to sterility supposedly caused by witches. The broom was used to apply hallucinogenic ointment to its rider. The besom/ broom is also frequently used to ritually cleanse spaces.

In the early days, and especially in Italy, brooms were made from three woods: ash, birch, and willow. In other cultures brooms consisted of six woods—birch, broom, hawthorn, hazel, rowan, and willow—with each tree's wood having magickal significance. In modern witchcraft, brooms may clear and cleanse a space before a ritual. In olden times before mass communication methods, brooms placed in strategic positions outside the home were a way of communicating one's whereabouts.

A Dictionary of Superstitions (1988) stated that people commonly placed a broom on a threshold before a guest entered. If she was a witch, she would not enter but rather make an excuse and journey on down the road.

Witch stones are said to contain a naturally occurring hole and are typically found near bodies of water or underground. If one becomes broken, it is believed to have used its power to save a life.

Talismans are considered to be powerful protection amulets, protecting the wearer from bad intentions and various forms of evil, curses, hexes, and harm. Some people even place them under pillows to prevent nightmares.

Acorns, found in the fall in abundance, have been used as good luck talismans and also for fertility and prosperity. Witches believe in carrying acorns for protection. Placing them on windowsills prevents lightning strikes, while placing them on windowsills during a full moon is believed to increase the prosperity of the household.

Fruits and flowers come with their own folklore and mythology. The blackberry, according to the ancient Celts, was magical. A broom made out of its bramble was meant to ward off evil; this was known as a witch's whisk. Smoke from burning the ends of the witch's whisk was used to cleanse spaces and homes. Blackberry was also believed to release animals and humans from baneful energies.

Wiccan Family Temple, Sabbat Mabon in Tompkins Square Park, 2019.
Reverend Starr RavenHawk

Cecil Williamson, an influential English neo-pagan warlock who lived until 1999, described the witch's whisk as "made of dried out blackberry stems and with the end bound to form a handle. Here in the south west when a witch decides to make magic she first selects a spot or place where she will work, be the chosen place inside or out. The next thing to be done is that of cleansing the chosen spot of all evil forces. This is where the bundle of black-berry twigs comes in. She sets a light to the twigs and with them smouldering, burning and making smoke, she dances and weaves her way in and around and around over and over again. So this is one might call it: 'a witch's devil scarer.'"

Blackberry pies are baked on Lughnasadh (August 1) as one of the favorite ways to celebrate summer harvest. Blackberries and their leaves have long been used in rituals to create wealth and prosperity.

Cornell University in Ithaca, upstate New York, offers a Medicinal Plants Certificate Program to educate on the thousands of uses of plant products. This intro course highlights medicinal plants and their benefits to treating illness. Topics of study include historical applications of plant-based medicine; plants for muscle, bones, and reproductive systems; plants for mental health and pain relief; plants for improving cardiovascular and respiratory health; plants promoting digestive and skin health; and boosting immunity with medicinal plants.

Some elements of women's attire, which we now take for granted, were in the past linked to witchcraft.

Believe it or not, lipstick actually at one time carried its own superstition—that of seducing men into marriage, thereby considered witchcraft—so it was banned in 1770 by the British Parliament.

Pockets in dresses were phased out in olden times since women had to prove they weren't witches carrying spells in there.

Rituals are an important part of witchcraft, intention, and manifesting, and a way to bend time and change outcomes of situations. Magic is worked through intent and intentions, good or bad, producing white or black magic.

Salt, known as a banishing herb to Native Americans and also to the ancient Celts, has been thought of as a witch repellant and advised to be carried out and about on Halloween. Derived from the Latin word *salus* (safety), salt seems to have given many cultures protection from evil entities.

In 1832, from *Gents Magazine*: "To neutralize the evil influence of witchcraft . . . when good housewives put their cream into the churn, they sometimes cast a handful of salt into the fire." Also from *Gents*: "He had standing regularly by his fireside a sack-bag of salt and of this he frequently took a handful, with a few horsenail stumps, and crooked pins, and casting them into the fire together, prayed to the Lord to torment all witches and wizards in the neigbourhood."

Donna Parish-Bishoff is a practicing Wiccan, paranormal investigator, author, and witch crafter. On her blog *Little Witchaus* (littlewitchhaus.com), where you can find items for sale and information on Wicca and paganism, she describes black salt: "Black salt is a very handy ingredient to have in your cupboard; it can be used for protection, banishing, and breaking hexes and can also be used for laying simple hexes and curses of your own. It's useful for driving away anything and everything from depression, nasty spirits, other magic workers."

BLACK SALT USES

In a dish, in a bag, or under the pillow to ward off bad dreams, unwanted watchers, or spirits. Cast a line across your door or window to cast out evil, to avoid the unwanted company. Reflects slander or jealousy to the sender. Use in bath water when depressed or feeling negative or angry.

Keep a jar of it at work to deflect gossip at work; carry a small pouch in your pocket, purse, etc. to ward off rude people, bullies.

BLACK SALT RECIPE

Many other black items used in the occult world are often associated with evil and dark magic by outsiders. Those within the craft know that black is powerful for the protection and cleansing of negative energy. Black salt can be used in everything from cleansing and protecting to hexes and war water to help protect you from those out to do you harm. While you can find culinary black salt, it is very different from the black salt you would get at the local witch's shop. It is easy to make your own black salt for magic.

- Sea salt or kosher salt
- Activated charcoal capsules
- Ashes from incense
- Mortar and pestle
- Glass jar for storage

Fill a bowl with kosher salt; place a bunch of incense sticks in the bowl of salt and light them. As they burn, the ashes will fall into the salt; blend the ashes into the salt and mix them, place in a jar, and keep that as black salt.

From Donna Parrish-Bishoff's *Little Witchaus* blog (www.littlewitchaus.com/black-salt)

Bells were often employed in homes to ward off evil. Bells hung on doors were believed to protect the home's inhabitants, and also believed to make flying witches fall to the ground. Bells have mostly been associated with angels and the divine, thus the opposite of witchcraft, being a crime against God. They were meant to repel witches, and the sound vibrations attributed to bells were believed to be magical. Therefore, bells have been incorporated into jewelry and clothing and placed on animals through the ages as talismans.

Conversely, there have also been stories of witches using bells in their magic. Small handbells have been known to be used in Wiccan and pagan rituals to enhance power. Think of bells as a signaling device for modern witches, used to banish negativity and protection, make a space sacred, and to call on the dead. One ring is used to start a spell, three rings to clear negativity, seven or twenty-one rings to call on the dead. Even though in olden times witches were always to blame for bad weather, modern witches have been known to use bells in the face of severe storms in hopes of dispersing that energy positively: "Lightning and thunder, I break asunder" (from the *Standard Dictionary of Folklore, Mythology and Legend*, 1949).

According to Paranormal Knowledge (paranormalknowledge.com),

The phrase "bell, book and candle" became associated with witches because the church believed them to be Devil-worshipers who should be excommunicated. . . . Since the fifth century C.E., Christian church bells have been ascribed a special magical potency to combat evil and chase off the wicked spirits that lurked on every church threshold. In the Middle Ages, on nights when witches were believed to be about, such as Samhain (All Hallow's Eve) and Beltane (also known as Walpurgisnacht), church bells were rung to keep the witches from flying over a village. The townspeople also turned out and added to the noise by banging on pots and pans and ringing their own bells. . . .

Thunder and lightning storms were believed to be the work of witches and demons, and church bells also would be rung at an approaching storm in an attempt to dispel it. At someone's death, the tolling of the church bells helped the departing soul on its way to heaven and prevented evil spirits from interfering with the journey. . . .

Bells have been used in rituals for summoning the dead. One such necromantic bell is that of Giradius. Eighteenth-century French instructions specified that the bell be cast from an alloy of gold, silver, fixed mercury, tin, iron and lead at the exact day and hour of birth of the person who intends to use it. The bell was to be inscribed with various astrological symbols and the magical words of Adonai, Jesus and the Tetragrammaton. The bell was to be wrapped in green taffeta and placed in the middle of a grave in a cemetery. It was to be left for seven days, during which time it absorbed certain vibrations and emanations. At the end of a week, the bell was properly "cured" for necromancy rituals.

Shelby Mattice, curator of the Bronck Museum (believed to be the Hudson Valley's oldest home), in giving a talk for Hudson's Fortnightly Club, explained some early Dutch beliefs. Evergreens were commonly planted near doors of dwellings since a witch could not enter unless she could count all of its leaves. Horseshoes nailed to doors were another way to keep witches out. During the Middle Ages, mistletoe was also hung in doorways as a way to keep witches at bay.

The witching hour is the time between 3:00 and 4:00 a.m., when the veil is thought to be thinnest between this world and the Netherworld. It's when witches are the most active (ghosts also) and black magic the most potent to carry out. In other words, a portal opens between the world we can see and the world we can't.

This hour, also known as the Devil's hour or the chime hour, may date back to the 1500s during a time when the Catholic Church forbade activities between 3:00 and 4:00 a.m. as a preventative measure against witchcraft and demonic duties. The 3:00 a.m. time is an inverse of the 3:00 p.m. time that Christ died, and so is believed to be an intent of mockery. This has also recently been mentioned in the 2013 movie *The Conjuring*.

A sigil is a symbol created for the purpose of a ritual. It is empowered with intention.

The pentagram and pentacle often get confused; the pentacle is the pentagram but within a circle. Dating as far back as 3000 BCE, the Greeks worshipped the pentagram as symbolic of perfection. The pentagram, or pentacle, represents water, earth, air, fire, and spirit and is important to pagans.

In German folklore, the apotropaic use of the pentagram meant this symbol prevented the Devil from leaving a room. Because the pentagram has so often been misinterpreted as a symbol of evil, many public schools in America during the 1990s attempted to ban students from wearing this symbol on clothing or jewelry, going as far as suspending many students from attending class. In 2000 this was determined to be a violation of the right to free exercise of religion. In 2007 the pentacle was added to the list of thirty-eight (at the time) approved religious symbols that can be placed on tombstones of veterans at Arlington National Cemetery, when lawsuits were settled between families and the United States government.

For the first five hundred years after the death of Jesus, both the pentagram and pentacle were prominent symbols of the Catholic Church, representing the five wounds of Jesus and the five joys Mary had of Jesus, and were incorporated in the architectural elements of churches.

Eliphas Lévi's *Dogme et Rituel de la haute magie* (1855–56 and 61, translated into English by A. E. Waite under the title *Transcendental Magic*) explains further:

> The Pentagram, which in Gnostic schools is called the Blazing Star, is the sign of intellectual omnipotence and autocracy. It is the Star of the Magi; it is the sign of the Word made flesh; and, according to the direction of its points, this absolute magical symbol represents order or

confusion, the Divine Lamb of Ormuz and St. John, or the accursed goat of Mendes. It is initiation or profanation; it is Lucifer or Vesper, the star of morning or evening. It is Mary or Lilith, victory or death, day or night. The Pentagram with two points in the ascendant represents Satan as the goat of the Sabbath; when one point is in the ascendant, it is the sign of the Saviour. By placing it in such a manner that two of its points are in the ascendant and one is below, we may see the horns, ears and beard of the hierarchic Goat of Mendes, when it becomes the sign of infernal evocations.

In nature we see the star shape by cutting an apple in half, and see it on the bottom of rowan tree flowers. The five-pointed star represented the Witches' Pyramid, or Four Powers of the Magus.

The Sigil of Baphomet was the foremost symbol of Satanism after Anton LaVey's use of it and his establishment of the Church of Satan in 1966.

The imagery of the sigil has also been attributed to the Knights Templar and Freemasonry. The five points were often thought to represent the five virtues of knighthood: fidelity, honesty, courtesy, prowess, and generosity.

Eric Vernor, who is also known by the pen name Corvis Nocturnum, is a warlock and author of several books on the occult. He has given numerous university talks on the misconceptions of Satanism and in 2010 was a consultant for A&E's *Paranormal States* on its "Satan's Soldier" episode; he was also interviewed in the October 2009 issue of *Penthouse* magazine on sex and Satanism.

The Sigil of Baphomet: the original "Samael/Lilith" version. Wikimedia Commons, Creative Commons; Author: Arbeiterreserve; Attribution: ShareAlike 4.0 International (CC BY-SA 4.0)

In 2011, on BET's *The Lexi Show*, Eric identified the differences between Satanism as a religion versus the misconceptions created in part by superstition and Hollywood.

He explained that the common misconception of Satanists is that they are immoral and harmful to people and animals, which is not correct. Their bible, he explained, differs from that of "thou shalt not" to being one of "do unto others," accountability of one's actions, but also pointed out that this is not a religion of turning the other cheek. Satanism is a religion of retribution for those who may wrong you. "We're not gluttonous but don't believe in abstinence either; but make no mistake, we don't condone substance abuse at all." In speaking of the pentagram or pentacle (as surrounded by a circle), he contrasted the upward star used by pagans (collecting from the Universe) with the downward star used by Satanists as meaning the world coming to the individual—putting yourself first.

The Devil has long been a symbol closely associated with witches in folklore, literature, and art. Who is the Devil? It depends on what religion you ask. There is no devil in the craft of witchcraft, which predates Christianity. "So many religions and governments are about control and power. The Church of Satan is about empowering the individual," says Eric. The Devil is "a mental construct," he says, a worldwide symbol of fear and control. "There are heroes and villains, with most people falling somewhere in between. Leave a legacy. Lead."

With the rise in popularity of the Church of Satan and the subsequent corresponding but unrelated reporting of serial killings in the media during the 1970s and 1980s, the Satanic Panic ensued. The pentagram and pentacle began to be misused by the media to become synonymous with evil, and people have feared and misinterpreted these symbols ever since.

Walpurgisnacht, one of the witches' most high times of the year, came with superstition. According to the Old Craft (theoldcraft.com), "Before they went to sleep on the Night of the Witches, they covered their body with these secret ointments, which gave them visions of fire, flying witches, and horned gods. In the Middle Ages, many witches testified to the sensation of flight given by some of these ointments that contained narcotics and poisonous herbs. The Inquisition tried to find out the recipes for these secret ointments, and the witches who confessed did so using code names for the ingredients they used. Ingredients like baby fat, bat blood, opium, and mandrake fed the imagination of the public that witches were evil creatures that kidnapped children to use them for their sabats."

Many cultures believed that a witch couldn't pass over cold iron, and therefore buried knives around their properties to keep witches away. Witch bottles containing rosemary and wine were meant to impale the witch on the leaves of the rosemary while drowning the witch in the wine.

RITUALS AND SPELLS FOR THE AMATEUR WITCH

Words have power from intent. There are words still in use today that many lack an understanding of how and where these words came from and the intent behind them.

Abracadabra meant "I will create when I speak," while *Avada Kedavra* meant "I will destroy as I speak." From ancient Aramaic, both are believed to have been used in spell work by witches. It can be written downwards in triangle form to rid one of evil. In ancient times, written downwards this way, it adorned jewelry worn as a protection amulet.

For some specific spells, I asked my friend, Hyde Park, New York, author and upstate witch Donna Parish-Bischoff, for her favorites and include some here, in her own words.

Cleansing Bath Ritual

In magic, you often hear of smudging yourself, objects, your home, to clear negativity. But you should get into the practice of cleansing ritual baths. It holds so many purposes and I will tell you why: You prepare your candles, your altar, the symbols to do spell work. When you do a ritual bath, you are clearing yourself of any negative roadblocks. You mentally feel refreshed and recharged. When you feel clearer, recharged, motivated, that energy goes into the spell work you perform.

You can create your own personalized bath soak but when cleansing, I always slice up citrus fruits and place the slices while the hot water is pouring into the tub: grapefruits, oranges, lemons, limes. Add sea salt, Epsom salt, or Himalayan pink salt.

When choosing the essential oils to drop in, you can create a combo of oils that correspond with the type of spell work you are performing. For example, if you are performing the money or love spell, you can add the following oils to your bath:

Money spell: frankincense oil, cinnamon oil, wild orange

Love spell: rosemary, lavender, ylang-ylang, amyris

To do this bath ritual, try to do it in quiet time. When everything is still, and you can allocate at least thirty minutes. And while you are soaking, visualize your spell as it has already come to fruition. You can make up a chant that has to do with your spell. If you are seeking finances, imagine yourself paying off all your bills and keep repeating, "I am debt free, and all is possible. All my debts are paid off."

The more personal you make the chant, use words that are already in motion as if they are happening already. When you are done with this bath, close it out by saying, "So mote it be!"

Love Spell

People often do love spells looking for others to instantly fall in love with them. But I have a problem with that. Be incredibly careful with what you ask for. It can turn sinister and nightmarish.

We need to accept ourselves, love ourselves, before we expect another person to come into our lives. If you love who you are, what you do, what you stand for, believe in, how you look, your style—stop being mean to yourself. Then you will find the spells you do will attract a like-minded soul that resonates with who you are.

So, after you have all of that in check, trust me, you won't be looking back a year from now thinking you have made a horrible mistake. Getting that off my chest, go grab your tools for this spell:

Pink candle

Gold candle for inner strength and to inspire self-realization

Rose quartz

Agate to bring you soothing strength

Rhodochrosite to inspire a loving positive attitude

Lavender essential oil or incense or dried lavender for bringing calming love and

    peace

Find a quiet space to arrange your items and light your candles. Holding all three stones, meditate on your life's journey up to this point. As the candles burn, think or meditate about your life—the challenges, the high points, and the low points. Look at all aspects of your life without judgment; simply be an observer. Think about three things you're grateful for that have happened in your life and say them aloud.

Say positive affirmations about your journey aloud; here are some examples: *I trust my journey, I love my life, my challenges strengthen me, I am open to learning from this life, I trust that I am right where I'm supposed to be.* Spend as much time as you'd like in quiet reflecting. Thank yourself for taking the time to offer yourself this love and blow out your candles. Keep your items up as a reminder if you'd like.

Money Spell

1 green candle (can be a green birthday candle if you are short on time)

Fireproof bowl (I use a large, deep stockpot, or use your cauldron if you have one)

6 coins

Cinnamon oil

A small green pouch or an 8-by-8 square of green fabric (you can be creative and
   DIY a pouch if you find a fabric with money on it: dollar signs, etc.)

Place your candle in the center of the bowl. Take the coins and make a circle around the candle.

Dress your candle with the cinnamon oil. Light the candle and sprinkle the fabric pouch with the cinnamon oil. Chant three times:

Money flow

Money grow

Money shine

Money mine

Now chant the following for a few minutes as you envision yourself with money:

Bring me money three times three

If you are using a larger candle that is still burning, you can snuff it out—*do not blow it out!*

Phobias

Believe it or not, there are many phobias related to witches and Halloween, so I thought I'd include some I came across. Phobias are a more intense type of fear that can be debilitating. Some of these phobias may be learned from bad experiences or spoken to us by an older relative, and phobias have also been thought to possibly stem from past lives.

Samhainophobia is the fear of Samhain, the festival of Halloween, fearing the Festival of the Dead believing it represents evil. To people who really don't like Halloween, the entire month of October leading up to it is a stressful time. I have met people along the way who do experience this fear—a form of anxiety, uneasiness, and tension until the day passes. And it is actually more common in children than adults. In my travels, I have noticed that many adults who relate to this phobia have had bad experiences with Halloween as children themselves. In modern times, when Halloween approaches, we are bombarded with its imagery where we work, live, and go to school and on television. A festive and colorful time for many, it is a time of dread for others.

Chiroptophobia is a severe and overwhelming fear of bats. Since bats are a classic symbol of Halloween, chiroptophobia is included in this list. People with chiroptophobia experience trembling, have an increased heart rate, begin sweating, and even run away when a bat is nearby. As a friend of mine used to say, "There's just no good way to look at a bat." In the summertime, when bats are mating and more active, it is common for them to find ways into people's homes, which is not pleasant.

Cucurbitophobia is the fear of pumpkins and is rare, but it does exist. For those of us who love anything Halloween, it can be hard to understand this fear, and all we can do is be compassionate.

Wiccaphobia is the fear of witches, and people still get anxious and fearful if they suspect a witch is nearby. Sometimes when people experience rough patches in life, they seek to blame someone or believe that someone has hexed or cursed them. In today's world, there are still misconceptions about witchcraft and Halloween, so it's no surprise that many of these have become actual phobias.

The list also includes:

Arachnophobia: fear of spiders
Astraphobia: fear of thunder and lightning
Bogyphobia: fear of the boogeyman
Lupophobia: fear of wolves and werewolves
Maskaphobia: fear of masks
Necrophobia: fear of dead things
Nyctophobia: fear of the dark
Phasmophobia: fear of ghosts
Placophobia: fear of tombstones
Sanguivoriphobia: fear of vampires
Selenophobia: fear of the moon
Skelephobia: fear of skeletons
Teraphobia: fear of monsters

So the next time you hear that someone doesn't particularly care for Halloween, you now may know why . . .

Rituals at Samhain. Photograph by Elizabeth Goodermote, Historic Nassau Preservation Committee, NYSDAR Fort Crailo Chapter Regent, e.goodermote_artist

WITCHES AND THE MOON

Just like many herbs and their correspondences, witches have long used the phases of the moon to intensify their spell work. It was discovered by our early ancestors long ago, the power that the moon has over the oceans and our growing seasons. Equally, spell work done with intention is most potent during certain phases of the moon.

The ancients were able to predict weather patterns based on moon phases, which was thought to be magic in itself. It is known that the moon affects our emotions, and it is believed that the moon rules our subconscious. The Triple Moon Goddess is seen frequently in jewelry, depicting the waxing, waning, and full moon phases, symbolic of the Maiden, the Mother, and the Crone archetypes.

New moon: A time when the moon is dark and not visible to us, this is a time for laying out plans, beginnings of all kinds, and planting seeds literally and figuratively.

Waxing moon: Viewed as what looks like a backwards *C*, this is a time of growth and starting to see the fruits of one's labors and setting intention, a good time for legalities and finances and exploring creativity.

Waxing gibbous: As the moon's energy wanes, this is a time for other things waning too, a time for minor magical work as the moon's energetic magic starts to later rebuild, a time to finish projects you've struggled with, a time also for mindfulness.

Full moon: This is the moon's most powerful phase where some witches make moon water by setting out a glass jar with water to be energetically charged and used in spell work, a time when secrets are revealed, a time to reap the harvest of your past intentions and actions.

Waning gibbous: A time for banishing rituals and letting go, clearing out the old, turning inwards, and rituals of gratitude.

Third quarter moon: Letting go, when the moon is roughly half visible and losing some of its power, a time to decide what needs to be removed from your life.

Waning crescent moon: The eighth and last phase of the moon, the right side is mostly dark, and those born during this phase are believed to have psychic abilities; a time to rest, recuperate, and surrender.

CURSES AND HEXES

The evil eye is something that ancient and modern witches are all too familiar with, and have remedies for. Called *il malocchio* in Italian, the evil eye is an ill-intended negative and harsh stare from someone, possibly stemming from jealousy or anger, and can come from anyone anywhere: neighbors, coworkers, or strangers on the street. Many cultures—Jewish, Greek, Egyptian, and Italian—for thousands of years have believed that the evil eye causes intended harm or puts a curse on the recipient. Throughout history, protective amulets have been created to wear in hopes of warding off the intended stare and the misfortune that can come after. Many of us know of this ancient belief from our grandparents.

Leanne Marrama, coauthor of the forthcoming *Lighting the Wick: An Intuitive Guide to the Ancient Art and Magic of Candles* and co-owner of Pentagram, a witchcraft shop in Salem, Massachusetts, has diagnosed the evil eye with a test for detecting its presence that utilizes olive oil and a bowl of water. "If the oil forms one large drop in the middle of the plate," she said, "then it is a sure sign of the evil eye."

Many cultures and families have their own methods of returning the evil eye's negative intent back to the sender. "My mother's side of the family and my father's side of the family had two different ways of identifying and busting the evil eye," Leanne explained. "My mother used scissors and my aunt used a silver steak knife. Other families use pins or razors stabbed directly into the oily eye, followed by three pinches of salt."

Leanne further illustrated the ritual through the lens of her own Italian heritage. She explained that a *strega*—an Italian witch—will "say secret words or simply the Hail Mary three times" to break or banish the negativity. "Often an egg is dropped into the bowl filled with water and oil," she added. "The egg absorbs the evil and is then tossed into the toilet."

Antonio Pagliarulo, of Manhattan, has been a member of the pagan community since his teens. He wrote *Rocking the Goddess: Campus Wicca for the Student Practitioner* (2002) and *American Witch: Magick for the Modern Seeker* (2003) under the pen name Anthony Paige and is also the author of five young adult novels. The son of Italian immigrants, Antonio was taught the ways of Italian folk magic and *stregheria*. He writes, "Among the practices that Jewish people have developed over the centuries are spitting three times after mentioning plans or positive developments, as seen in films like *Fiddler on the Roof*, or wearing a variety of different kinds of amulets for protection. These can include a hamsa, a hand-shaped shield that is sometimes cast with a jeweled eye in its center. It is called the hand of Fatima or Miriam, depending on the wearer, and is said to originate from the Muslim world and was also adopted by Jews who hail from that part of the world. Terms like *bad juju* and *negative energy* are used colloquially, and each is rooted in what the evil eye ultimately represents."

Many cultures use frankincense and myrrh incense and salt baths to clear and remove harmful energies. Magical practitioners have grown in recent decades, and so have witches, pagans, and folk practitioners on the spiritual plane of our existence.

Antonio has also written about and interviewed witches on the controversy over cursing and hexing. Practitioners believe in harming no one, but also restoring balance when wrongs need to be righted. "I think that when done for the right reasons, it's not wrong to perform curses," said Kate Freuler, author of *Of Blood and Bones: Working with Shadow Magick & the Dark Moon* (2020). "Cursing is a form of self-defense and protection in many cases, so in that context, I consider it ethical. I also strongly believe that when someone is actively harming you or disrupting your life, there's no reason to think you have to just lie down and take it. Standing up for yourself and fighting back is not unethical."

Antonio believes that "Freuler's book explores shadow magick, which encourages practitioners to delve more deeply into the realms of soul and psyche so that they can access a richer source of personal power. *Of Blood and Bones* includes tips on how to ethically use animal parts, bones, and blood in spells and rituals."

For so long, witches were thought to *only* curse and hex and to be generally malevolent, so modern witches had refrained from talking openly and publicly about engaging in cursing and hexing. These days it is different, with more awareness being raised on subjects like protection, self-defense, and mental health.

Antonio stated, "There has been a discernible shift in the way many witches relate to cursing; it is no longer taboo to broach the subject or admit to partaking in the practice. Adherents of traditional witchcraft, as well as those who classify their rites as 'eclectic' or completely detached from a specific tradition, see the Witch as a mirror of nature—unencumbered and a force unto itself. The Witch cannot be tamed, nor can the energy that fuels magic. The paradigm shift has created a more inclusive space for discourse and exploration." Again, it is the intention that becomes important in distinguishing between a protection spell and a curse.

In 2017, there was a worldwide movement to hex and curse the then-president of the United States. The hope was to bring about huge, positive social changes and all were encouraged to participate, made easier by the increased connectivity through social media. Magical supplies are also easier than ever to get in modern times thanks to the internet and fast delivery, although there are still many who enjoy the in-person experience of shopping in New York's magic supply shops; there are at least thirteen in upstate's Syracuse alone.

Magic isn't just spells and potions. It has power because you believe it does.

—*Sally,* Practical Magic

Witches and Warlocks
in Folklore and Film
in New York

HULDA THE WITCH OF SLEEPY
HOLLOW AND TARRYTOWN

America's first published ghost story, "The Legend of Sleepy Hollow," originated in the Hudson Valley, so let's start there—the Northeast place that Washington Irving referred to as "this spellbound region" that "still continues under the sway of some witching power."

From this book sprang the Headless Horseman, America's terrifying icon and archetype of horror that practically gives the Hudson Valley ownership of the Halloween season and a truly American-made experience. As described by the Reformed Church of the Tarrytowns on their website, "When Washington Irving set his ghost story about the Headless Horseman at the Old Dutch Church of Sleepy Hollow, he made the church world-famous. Ever since the publication of 'The Legend of Sleepy Hollow' in 1819–20, visitors have come to see where Ichabod Crane led the choir and courted Katrina Van Tassel among the old gravestones in the churchyard, and looked for the grave of the Headless Horseman in the Old Burying Ground. The church was already old when Irving first saw it, when he was a teenager. It was built in 1685 and formally organized as Dutch Reformed in 1697." In 1996 North Tarrytown renamed itself Sleepy Hollow.

"Tarrying," the act of staying longer than is intended, is quite possibly how Tarrytown got its name. The Headless Horseman is believed to be based on an actual Hessian soldier who having lost his head on the battlefield of the American Revolution due to a cannonball on the actual date of Halloween, would have been buried without a head, without a tombstone, in lands haunted by Indian and witch curses. His spirit would be doomed to remain restless and wander for eternity.

According to the website Occult World, Hulda in Teutonic folklore "presides over a transit station for human souls, a crossroads between life and death." She appears as a female from the front but as a tree from behind, and the winter solstice is considered her feast day. In *Chronicles of Tarrytown and Sleepy Hollow* (1897), author Edgar Mayhew Bacon states that local mothers would utter Hulda's name to scare their children into submission.

Since Colonial times, the Northeast's famous folklore of Hulda the Witch has been passed down through generations, and she's become known worldwide for a number of reasons.

Was she a white witch? A green witch? A solitary witch? An herbal goddess? A gypsy?

Her story is a fascinating example of individuality and courage. Hulda lived a solitary life in her cottage in the woods, practicing herbal remedies and bartering for supplies as needed with the area's Native Americans, having learned their language as well. Believed to be from Bohemia, she was described as having long flowing hair. She was possibly a widow when she settled near the Old Dutch Church Graveyard and Tarrytown in the 1700s. Her neighbors were warned in church not to talk to her. She was shunned. She was different. People are always afraid of the unknown and special knowledge.

Despite the hurts enacted upon her, Hulda was seemingly interested in helping others and was known to leave baskets of her herbs and other healing treatments on doorsteps when learning of neighbors' illnesses.

Washington Irving had learned of Hulda while visiting the region, her home being very near to the bridge mentioned in the "Legend of Sleepy Hollow" story, where Ichabod Crane evades the Headless Horseman's frightening offering of his own thrown head. He had claimed in his story that Sleepy Hollow was bewitched by a high German doctor, and many believe that Hulda is who he was referring to.

By the time she had settled in the Hudson Valley region, inhabitants were familiar with the name Hulda, which has its roots in German pagan mythology as a woods goddess with powers and knowledge of weather, weaving, and witchcraft. By then, this knowledge was popularized in a Brothers Grimm fairy tale, "Mother Hulda."

Speaking to the *Hudson Independent* newspaper in 2017, Sara Mascia, executive director of the Historical Society, Inc., of Tarrytown and Sleepy Hollow, said, "These stories were discussed a great deal in the last century and then disappeared with the advent of TV as people turned from oral legend to television entertainment. In recent years, there has been a resurgence of interest in our local witch stories as these stories have been dramatically narrated in The Old Dutch Church, and celebrated by self-professed witches and tourists alike, particularly around Halloween."

By the late 1800s, little had been written or documented of Hulda. But thanks to friend and colleague Jonathan Kruk and his book *Legends and Lore of Sleepy Hollow and the Hudson Valley* (2011) and the work of other historians beginning in the 1970s, Hulda has not been lost to time.

We know from many sources that she had been prohibited from joining up with the Continental Army during the Revolutionary War. Remarkably, she was not burned at the stake or hanged, but rather died a hero of the war for leading Redcoats away from the village not long after their landing on the shores near Tappan Zee. Stray gunshot was perhaps her downfall.

According to *Chronicles of Tarrytown and Sleepy Hollow,*

In those days, men patrolled the highways to intercept the cattle-thieves that ran off their stock, and as the population became smaller, the women sometimes took their places with flint-lock and powder-horn. Hulda, the witch, presented herself for this service, but no one wanted her companionship. At last one day a force of British landed from one of the transports that had sailed up the Hudson and commenced a march which was to bring them, by means of the King's highway, to the rear of Putnam's position, at Peekskill. As they marched in imposing array a volley greeted them from behind walls and tree-trunks.

It was Lexington repeated in Westchester County. Not to be repulsed this time, Hulda fought with her neighbors, using her rifle with great effect, so that she was singled out for vengeance; and before the redcoats retreated to their boats they had, by means of a sortie, overtaken and killed the witch.

Even more remarkably, Hulda was later given a burial in the Old Dutch Burial Ground, although without a headstone as was the custom in those days if a person was unbaptized or considered an outcast. She remains an interesting figure to this day, considered a white witch for her practices and beliefs of harming no one.

Marie Lizzeau, who showed me Hulda's final resting place, stated with pride, "On August 15, 2019, Hulda was finally given a headstone in a prominent place in the cemetery of the Old Dutch Church of Sleepy Hollow, New York. Today I was happy to pay my respects to her wearing my 100% That Witch shirt. Mother Hulda's tombstone reads: 'Healer. Herbalist. Patriot.' I don't have any moral to offer for this story, but I'm glad that she finally received the respect that she deserves." The beautiful stone carving of Hulda's tombstone was created by restoration expert Robert Carpenter.

Each and every time we write about Hulda, hopefully many new people will learn of her existence. In October 2021, the *Albany Times Union* published a story on Hulda. In it, Carla L. Hall, a practicing witch in Ossining researching folk magic, said, "As soon as Hulda's gravestone was announced in August 2019, I was fascinated with the story. That October I found myself retelling her story at her gravesite to anyone who'd listen." Carla then created a production, *Hulda: The Other Legend of Sleepy Hollow*, to be held at the Old Dutch Church. The play was told from the perspective of Abby, an African girl based on Carla's research into the enslaved people who lived at Philipsburg Manor and built the Old Dutch Church. In Carla's story, Abby meets Hulda at a time when both of these women would have been forced to live on the edges of society.

Becoming a folk hero, Hulda will forever remain in the hearts of many upstate New Yorkers.

The late Joe Netherworld, a Poughkeepsie witch—he preferred to be known as a witch as opposed to a warlock—talks about Hulda and her origins in Bohemia in his YouTube video, "Wicked Witches." Joe was also a beloved member of the pagan community, and luckily we have his very entertaining video not only to remember Hulda but also to remember him by.

Krystal Madison, the "Witch of Sleepy Hollow," told *Westchester Woman* magazine that "2014 was the first year for Festival of Witches, which I created to both celebrate Hulda's life as well as bridge the gap between the Pagan/Witch community and the local communities in which we live and work. I felt that her story and her legacy didn't garner the attention it deserved. She died a hero and was given the honor (for the time) of a proper burial in the church grounds of a community that had essentially shunned her in life. I also created it to show others that witches *are* real, and we are here to serve our communities." Hulda is also honored annually with Hulda's Night, held by the Rockefeller Preserve.

There is a beautiful YouTube video, "The Witch of Sleepy Hollow," about Hulda from September 2019 that gives a little of her history and reminds us to respect the dead and their graves, which "are not Halloween props."

Tombstone of Hulda the Witch, Sleepy Hollow, New York. Courtesy of Reformed Church of the Tarrytowns and Reneelyn Chillemi

Upon her death, Hulda was carried back to her hut home, where she kept a Bible. Within it was a will leaving a small amount of gold to village widows who had lost their husbands to the war; even after death, Hulda was carrying on with being helpful to her neighbors. It didn't take long for hearts to soften and people to realize that she deserved a proper resting place, but only much later (two hundred years later), in 2019, did Hulda finally receive a headstone.

Each year Sleepy Hollow receives tens of thousands of visitors seeking out the landscapes where "The Legend of Sleepy Hollow" and Hulda's life took place. She is still remembered in church services nearby. Old Dutch Church docent Deb McCrue recalls, "On Reformation Sunday, Oct 27th, Rev. Jeff Gargano recalled the persecution of Hulda of Bohemia and dedicated the memorial marker that now binds her story to the story of The Old Dutch Church. As head docent of the church and burying ground, I was asked to offer a remembrance during the service. Hulda's headstone is carved in the style of John Zuricher, a prolific stone carver in the mid-18th century whose work can be found in numerous burying grounds crossing all denominations. It was decided that Hulda's memorial should be in the style of her day. The soul effigy is a colonial symbol that the soul has ascended to heaven." The tombstone was funded through the Friends of the Old Dutch Burying Ground.

You can visit Hulda's home and tombstone by contacting the area historical society. See also visitsleepyhollow.com for more local legends and information.

HOUDINI AND THE OCCULT

An ordinary life shackles us.

—Harry Houdini

People as legendary as Harry Houdini remain fascinating long after they've departed. You have to marvel at their appeal. In the late 1800s, Harry and his family left Milwaukee and a life of poverty for New York. Showbiz enticed him away from an ordinary life, and in the early 1900s he would know great fame and fortune.

Poster for the Houdinis' show, circa 1895. Library of Congress; Liebler & Maass Lith., New York

Known for his magic tricks and escape artistry, Houdini later in his career engaged vigorously in exposing séances and also clairvoyants, tarot card readers, and psychics—those who fell under the category of witches—as frauds. Houdini railed against the new religion "spiritualism," which mushroomed in the 1920s. He was outraged by those making money off of people grieving their lost loved ones, including the vast numbers of war dead from the Civil War and World War I. Harry attended many séances in disguise, recognized many common parlor tricks, and waited for that dramatic moment when he could reveal his identity and the fraudster by saying, "I'm Harry Houdini and you're a fraud!" By continually exposing many spiritualists as frauds, Houdini started receiving death threats and having curses thrown at him.

After tirelessly engaging in the debunking of the spiritualists and mediums of his day, Houdini vowed that if there was a way to communicate from the Great Beyond, he would do so. He became obsessed with the afterlife following the death of his beloved mother in 1913 and began contacting psychics and mediums to attempt communication with her, only to be continually disheartened upon learning of their parlor tricks and the type of stage magic that he knew all too well from his own performances. He proceeded to make a name for himself as he traveled about calling upon psychics to prove themselves and their powers live and onstage. By 1922 he had joined the *Scientific American* panel offering $2,500 cash to any true medium able to offer real proof of spiritualism. Many tried, but none could pass the tests put forth by the panel.

Harry Houdini had first made a name for himself in the 1890s, capturing the public's fascination by being an escape artist. One of his feats was to be chained to a wooden crate then tossed into New York's East River. The public gasped, and Houdini always managed to escape. The Water Torture Cell was where he'd be locked in chains, hung by his ankles, and lowered into the glass tank, which was seemingly impossible to escape. The public watched in fascination and horror while a clock ticked away, but Houdini always managed to escape. He courted and cheated death on numerous occasions. He was during his life one of the world's most famous performers.

Houdini would also be remembered for one of the greatest love stories in modern times. In 1894 he married the love of his life, singer and dancer Beatrice Raymond, or "Bess," as he would call her. Between them, they created a code known only to them for Harry to prove after his death that there was an afterlife, if there was one. It would spell out "Rosabelle Believe," but in a complicated way that would end up with that message. "Rosabelle" was a song they both loved from the time they fell in love at Coney Island; it was later engraved into the ring he gave her.

Arthur Ford was convinced to become a medium by Sherlock Holmes creator Sir Arthur Conan Doyle. Ford, a skeptic, had become known for having precognitive dreams while in the service during World War I. It was Ford who would conduct the séance with Houdini's widow in their home in 1929, three years after Houdini's death on Halloween. Thomas Razzeto provides exhaustive research demonstrating that there is a reasonable chance of this case being genuine. Ford not only revealed the entire secret message but also explained the decoding method of the ten key words, with details of decoding this message. He stated that this was only possible because of the presence of Houdini and his mother.

Houdini's widow confirmed the correctness of the message with several witnesses present. She gave an interview that night to the *New York Times*, signing a statement along with H. R. Zander of the United Press and John W. Stafford, associate editor of *Scientific American.* "They are the exact words left for me by Harry and I am absolutely convinced that my husband talked to me and that there is life beyond the grave," she said. It should be noted that Mrs. Houdini was going against "the grain of peer acceptance" at the time, since none of her family or friends believed this was possible, and that neither she nor Harry believed in spirit communication. She later wrote a letter to famed columnist Walter Winchell attesting to the validity of the séance and its message.

The *New York Times* reported in January 1929 that no one but Houdini and his widow could possibly have known the details of the code because of its complexity. Fourteen months later, however, the *Times* reported that Houdini's widow was now denying the message of the séance, stating she was giving up on hopes of communication from Harry. We can only speculate, but her social circles may have played a part in her retraction. She would, however, continue to hold high-profile séances on Halloween for the next five years. Her last séance was held in 1936, where she concluded the radio broadcast by saying, "Turn out the light. Goodnight, Harry. Ten years is long enough to wait for any man."

In 1923, Valatie's Beaver Kill Falls was a location for one of Harry's films, *Haldane of the Secret Service.* The Houdini Picture Corporation made many silent films, several depicting his escapes, some of which still remain unexplainable to this day.

There have been séances every year since Houdini's death in hopes of contacting him.

Death is the uninvited dinner guest at the banquet of life.

—*Kiran Aldridge*

THE CATSKILL WITCH

The 1970s out-of-print book by James McMurry, *The Catskill Witch and Other Tales of the Hudson Valley*, remains a favorite book on upstate New York folklore. The book is illustrated by Jeff Jones, a prominent New York illustrator who passed away in May of 2001 after a successful career from the 1960s to 2000s in book cover and comic book illustration. The illustrations in *The Catskill Witch* are in pen and ink, which the author described to me as being not exactly what he had hoped for, since he had wanted illustrations in color.

In describing his inspiration to write the book, James said, "Not long after coming to live within view of the beautiful Hudson River I discovered a book of tales entitled *Myths and Legends of Our Own Land* by Charles M. Skinner. The first volume of this once-popular collection contains sundry legends of the Hudson and its Hills. So enchanted was I by these fanciful tales I decided many of them should be kept alive by being retold in more modern idiom and with some embellishment. Then, to the stories found in Skinner, I added nine of my own making, drawing freely from New York folk and Indian lore, from literature, from history and, of course, from imagination."

McMurry's wonderful storytelling and prose makes this book vividly lovely for children as well as adults. In it, he modified an old Indian tale also known to Washington Irving. Originally known as "The Old Squaw of the Mountains," the Dutch updated the tale to "The Catskill Witch."

The Catskill Witch, spinning black clouds and flinging them to the winds. By her side was a pile of magic gourds. She cast them one by one against the rocks, and torrents of water burst forth down the mountainside and fell as thundershowers from the skies round about. As she spun the dark clouds and broke the gourds, the Witch sang to herself:

Blow, blow, winds of ice,

Down the mountain pass;

Thunder and lightning

Rumble and roar,

And darkness fill the air

Til gone is all weather fair.

Never had Solomon Brink seen so ill-omened a sight in all his life, and the fear in his heart bade him turn back from his foolhardy adventure. But his determination to avenge himself on the Witch for her deceitful tricks and his curiosity to see more closely how she spun the clouds and made the rain fall goaded him on. So he climbed higher yet up the mountain. But at just that moment, the Witch turned and saw him. She looked him full in the face and said with a terrible gleam in her eye, "You are too curious a man, Solomon Brink! Have you come for your trophy? Then you shall have it!" And picking up the largest of the magic gourds, she dashed it on the rocks where he stood. The last thing poor Solomon heard was the Witch's scream of laughter, for the gourd burst before him, and a spring welled up in such volume the unhappy man was engulfed in its waters. He was swept to the edge of Kaaterskill Clove and dashed on the rocks two hundred and sixty feet below. Nor did the water from the magic gourd ever cease to run, and in these times, the stream born of the Witch's revenge is known as Catskill Creek. When his friend failed to return, Rip and Wolf made their way back home, alone and sorrowful. He was not one to meddle with the Catskill Witch and risk the loss of his soul; and yet some say it was to search for Solomon Brink that Rip Van Winkle went into the mountains a week later. But that time, Rip met with other adventures, as we all know well.

In Palenville, Greene County, we know from the Delaware Historical Society that this old tale was also known as "The Witch of Kaaterskill Clove." According to the local Indians, nearby mountain peaks were home to this witch who controlled the weather. Of course, anyone who displeased or disrespected her would bear the brunt of violent storms. Encountering her was a sure way to get lost in the local woods.

WITCHES OF THE CATSKILLS

When Washington Irving described the Catskills as "this spell-bound region" it was among America's earliest known settlements, with, of course, witch tales of its own. Delaware, Greene, Otsego, Schoharie, Sullivan, and Ulster Counties had their fair share of witchcraft accusations.

Folklore and mythology were woven into the fabric of our past among a melting cauldron of people—Native Americans, Dutch, and other immigrants—bringing with them their superstitions and belief systems, as well as some international flavors from writers like Washington Irving himself. Witches of the Catskills were largely blamed for issues common at the time throughout America's early agricultural communities, including livestock problems, cream production or lack thereof, and unfavorable weather.

The Austin Witch wasn't named for an actual accused witch, but was called that after the Austin family of Trout Creek, Delaware County, thought they had been the target of bewitching by a witch somewhere nearby. Strange happenings included Mrs. Austin repeatedly finding a Sunday dress tattered, even after she locked the garment

Catskill Forest; photograph probably by James Hunter (d. 1896). Library of Congress

away after mending it, wearing the key so no one else had access to it. Butter barrels in the basement seemed to have been tampered with, with butter smeared on the basement walls, and liquid-filled barrels outside were found upside down. Mr. Austin's hay knife was found in the barn so high up that he needed a ladder to fetch it.

Believing like so many others that witches could not pass under steel, the Austin family placed steel sewing needles over every doorway into the house and within the house, after which they noticed no more bewitching activities befalling them. William and Harriet Austin died in 1903 and 1908, respectively, and are buried in the Trout Creek Cemetery.

In Delhi, Delaware County, in the late 1800s there were myths of a dwarf race of people living there and also in Sullivan County, supposedly ruled over by a witch called "Mom Spicer." Her clan allegedly numbered in the two hundred range, with the dwarves having a distinctly unpleasant smell.

One source for this folklore came from an article by W. H. Lyman for *The Illustrated American* magazine, "A Race of American Dwarves," on June 20, 1896. These upstate New York dwarves supposedly had traits in common with similar dwarves called Cagnots who lived in France during the Middle Ages.

The Delhi dwarf women were feared to also be witches, able to use the occult to harm anyone who crossed them. There is no factual evidence of this, but the "Mom Spicer" character was thought to have been an actual person working as a fortune teller traveling throughout New York State.

In Milford, Otsego County, a woman named Mrs. McGraw was accused of being a witch by her neighbor Mrs. Dingman, who attempted to stone her. Fortunately Mrs. Dingman was arrested and ordered to pay restitution to Mrs. McGraw, which ended the nonsense.

From the 1939 book *Body, Boots & Britches: Folktales, Ballads, and Speech from Country New York* by Harold Thompson to 2019's *Witches of the Catskills* by Samantha Misa, stories of bewitched cats are recorded. A folklorist named Emelyn Gardner in 1937 had also been acquiring stories of witchcraft and many of them pertained to cats. Cats with eyes like "coals of fire," mutilations of cats, and cats shot with silver bullets disappearing were common.

Molly Meyers, the so-called Witch Cat of South Gilboa, Schoharie County, is a weird tale recounted by Samantha Misa: "The story begins with a man identified only as Mr. Williams, who worked as a hired hand on the Cornelius Mayham farm. Mr. Williams was walking through Spook Woods one night when he suddenly realized he wasn't alone. Two cats were walking through the woods carrying a dead cat between them. One of the cats called out to him, 'Mr. Williams, tell Molly Meyers she can come home now; old Hawkins is dead.' When Mr. Williams spoke of this to the family he worked for, the family cat allegedly flew up the chimney, never to be seen again."

Also in Schoharie County was the tale of a "Witch Schermerhorn." She was accursed of the usual misfortunes that befell her neighbors: livestock, milk not churning into butter or cream, killing of fish in nearby waterways, and failing apple trees. Some partridge hunters not having luck also reported that Miss Schermerhorn appeared to them in the woods with holes in her wrists. Other hunters allegedly heard birds talking to one another, which she was accused of also bewitching.

In 1892, the *Delaware Gazette* published an article titled "Witches and Witchery: Early Days in the Delaware and Neversink Valleys Recalled" about the continued belief in witchcraft.

Near what is now New Paltz, Avery Hornbeck believed he was being abducted during his sleep by witches, used as a flying means, and taken to their sabbats. Many scholars have written of abduction stories in the twentieth and twenty-first centuries focusing on alien/UFO encounters, while in our country's early days the belief in curses and witchcraft was strong and pervasive in daily life.

Greg Newkirk manages a website called Week in Weird (weekinweird.com) where he writes about an interesting artifact from early upstate New York in 2016; a strange carving found in a cave believed to be fashioned from the "Old Meg" hermit queen who once lived in the woods of Sullivan County. He stated: "Several months ago, I received an email from a frightened New York man who believed he had come into possession of a cursed object causing terrifying poltergeist manifestations in his friend's home. The artifact was a crude, hand-carved effigy of a woman, with a stained noose hung around its neck and rusty nails hammered into its eyes. He and a friend had discovered the figure hidden in a cave while hiking in the Catskill Mountains, and despite his objections, his hiking partner decided to bring it home. After the frightening manifestation of an old woman, soaking wet, appeared crouched in the dark shadows of the living room, they knew they needed to seek help."

The man who had disturbed the statue and brought it into his home then called his hiker friend and told him that the object kept moving into different places in his house and he was noticing strange smells not encountered before. On Greg's website you can see a picture of the statue as it had apparently been found within the Catskill cave.

Once the man went public with his find and his strange household occurrences, he received a variety of advice, including the admonishment that he never should have disturbed the object in the first place. Given our country's melting pot even in the early days, some thought the object pertained to voodoo.

During the first week that the object resided in his home, the disturbances also started to include banging and loud knocks that would wake him from a sound sleep, and each time upon being woken up he experienced the strong smell of pond water. "Last night someone knocked on his door at three in the morning, but when he went to open it there was no one there. His motion lights weren't on and there weren't any cars in his driveway," Greg recounts from testimony of the man's concerned friend. We know from folklore that 3:00 a.m. is considered the witching hour.

As the disturbances intensified, agitating also his dog, both he and his dog wound up leaving and staying at his hiker friend's house—both trying to find a solution and an end to what they had apparently unleashed. Through the internet, they reached out for help, and their pleas were picked up by Greg, who advised them to return the object to exactly where they had found it.

So both men and the dog returned to the house to retrieve the object in hopes of returning it to the Catskills cave: "Today we went back to my friend's house to get the statue and return it. When we got there, I saw the muddy footprints he was talking about and the whole place smelled like a dog that had just rolled around in the dirt. His dog wouldn't even come in the house. When we were standing in the hallway talking to this thing his dog started barking like crazy outside and when we went to see what was going on, we both thought we saw a woman standing in the dark corner of his living room. She was totally naked, really old, and dripping water, and her eyes sort of glowed in the dark. She was hunched over near his shelves."

Since what they claimed to have experienced was terrifying to them, they did not even want to return the object to the cave. They instead sent it to Greg to be included in the Traveling Museum of the Paranormal & Occult.

"With the paranormal, intention is everything," explained Greg. "I can't stress this enough. If you go into a haunted location intending to have a scary, aggressive experience, you'll probably have one. If you intend to commune with the peaceful spirits residing in the location, you'll more than likely have a peaceful experience. The same goes for magick. With just a cursory glance, it's easy to see that someone focused a lot of time, energy, and *intent* into the creation of The Crone. It was carved by hand, probably with a very specific purpose in mind. Every rusty nail received a mental command as it was hammered into the figure's wooden eye-sockets. The noose around its neck was tied with a hidden desire in mind."

Once Greg received the object, he could see firsthand some of what had been conveyed to him by the hiker, as he experienced his own strange happenings. In the room where the object was kept, both Greg and his wife heard commotion on some occasions and discovered some objects moved. A camera subsequently placed in the room captured subtle movement of the object, seemingly moving on its own. Greg and his wife experienced the pungent smell of pond water and found water spots on some of their furniture without explanation.

So, getting back to "Old Meg" of Sullivan County—she was believed to be an eighteenth-century witch, over six feet tall, and had the ability to tell fortunes. Her tale had been retold in the 1940 book *New York: A Guide to the Empire State.* When Meg seemed to have disappeared from the county, allegedly a hunter found her body impaled on a splintered tree stump. Legend has it that this hunter brought two hundred people together to hold a wake for Old Meg, subsequently burning down her cabin for closure. Samantha Misa and the Delaware County Historical Association are credited for documenting witchcraft stories in very remote parts of upstate New York, some going back to the 1700s.

All these years later, The Crone, as the object found in the cave began to be called, toured with the traveling museum dedicated to the paranormal, so that the public could see the object for themselves. Visitors experienced negative side effects from viewing the object, almost as if it was cursed. The Travel Channel's regular guest and "acclaimed psychic Chip Coffey wanted to straight up exorcise the figure with holy water blessed by the Pope himself," said Greg.

The object is not allowed to be touched, and its purpose is still a mystery. "My own personal belief is that The Crone was created as an attempt to summon the spirit of a local witch for purposes unknown. The location of its discovery, coupled with the specifics of the carving's creation, leads me to believe that someone was aiming to commune with—and contain—a particular spirit," said Greg.

Maybe someday we can acquire more knowledge of "Old Meg" and the object known as The Crone. In the meantime, this story is another example of the caution that people should exercise in finding and handling objects that may have been used for ritual purposes.

Slave folklore in the 1800s written about in a *Tri-States Union* article titled "Witches of Years Ago," which retells a tale from a slave named Old Tashee about a woman living near the Delaware River in a cabin who supposedly was in contract with the Devil, giving her witchcraft powers of afflicting cattle and cursing those who wronged her. Ulster County also has tales of "spook holes" where witches would hide and attack travelers.

It's no surprise then that the only recourse against witches available to folks throughout New York State started to come in the form of witch doctors. E. H. Benjamin, Dr. Bartholomew, Dr. Brink, and Dr. Moulter of the Schoharie Hills area made money curing local folks afflicted by witchcraft. Dr. Brink also supposedly could cure uncooperative ships and boats along the Hudson River, including a boat in Catskill believed to be possessed by a witch, where he used witch-hazel and elder to rid the vessel of her.

THE WITCH TRIALS OF KATHERINE HARRISON

There is some conflicting information on Katherine Harrison's life. Some accounts such as Wikipedia state that it was only after becoming widowed that her witchcraft troubles began as the last

convicted witch in Wethersfield, Connecticut, in 1669; accounts
state that her husband's death was pivotal because beforehand she

MATTHEW HOPKINS,
OF MANNINGTREE, ESSEX,
THE CELEBRATED WITCH-FINDER.

FROM A VERY RARE PRINT IN THE PEPYSIAN LIBRARY, AT
MAGDALENE COLLEGE, CAMBRIDGE.

Matthew Hopkins of Manningtree, Essex, England, the "celebrated witch-finder." Hopkins actively hunted witches in the years 1644–46 and is believed to be responsible for the executions of over one hundred alleged witches. Public domain image; Division of Rare and Manuscript Collections, Cornell University Library had never been accused. Moving to Westchester, New York, in 1670, she was subjected to new accusations of being a witch. But according to the *New York History* blog, Katherine had only been in America, from England, for less than twenty years before being accused of witchcraft by her Connecticut neighbors, arrested, and then jailed for a year, during which time her husband passed away. Her status as a newly wealthy widow may have contributed to jealousy and rumor, perhaps in either or both states.

We know from William Renwick Riddell, "Witchcraft in Old New York," *Journal of the American Institute of Criminal Law and Criminology* (1928–29), that:

> In a publication by the State of New York: Minutes of the Executive Council of the Province of New York . . . 1668, 1673, Albany, 1910, appears a case of alleged Witchcraft:
>
> In the "Towne of West Chester" in 1670 lived a woman, Katharine Harrison, widow of John Harrison of Wethersfield, Connecticut, whose daughter, Rebeckah, had married Josiah Hunt, son of Thomas Hunt, Sr., a man of some importance in the Town: Mrs. Harrison lived with this daughter and son-in-law. She had had an unfortunate history: born in England, she came to America about 1651 and settled in Wethersfield, where she married in 1653. On complaint made, she was arrested for Witchcraft in 1669 and after being in prison some twelve months she was placed on her trial for that offense at Hartford, Connecticut. She was found Guilty by the Jury; the Court did not agree with this finding; and May 20,

1670, the following Order was made: "Cort. of Assistants Harford, May 20th, 1670. This Cort. having considered ye Verdict of ye Jury respecting Katharine Harrison cannot concurre with them soe as to Sentence her to Death or to a longer Continuance in Restraint, but doe dismisse her from her Imprisonmt., Shee paying her just flees to ye Goaler; Willing her to minde ye performance of her Promise of removing from Weathersfield wch. is that, as will tend most to her own Safety and ye Contentmt. of the People who are her Neighbours. Daniell Garrad is allowed for Keeping Goodwife Harryson five pounds."

Upon coming to New York, we know from this source what may happened in regards to witchcraft accusations against Katherine:

She came to Westchester and lived with Josiah Hunt and his young, 16-year-old, wife, Rebeckah with whom she became involved in litigation over some property which the young woman claimed had been left her by her deceased father. It may be that this litigation had something to do with the charge made against her the same year.

Once the accusation was made, Katherine's troubles began here in New York:

"Ye Fort… Before the Governor," Colonel Francis Lovelace, a complaint made by "Thomas Hunt Senr. and Edward

Waters on behalf of ye Towne of West Chester against a woman suspected for a Witch who they desire may not live in their Towne" came on for hearing. Mrs. Harrison appeared "with Capt. Ponton to justify her selfe."

Her unfortunate experiences in Connecticut were rehashed in New York and an order made by Lovelace:

"Whereas Complaint hath beene made unto me by ye Inhabitants of West Chester agt. Katherine Harrison, late of Weathersfeild in his Maties. Colony of Conecticott, widow. That countrary to ye consent & good liking of ye Towne she would settle amongst them, & she being reputed to be a person lyeing undr. ye Suspiccon of Witchcraft hath given some cause of apprehension to ye Inhabitants there, To ye end their Jealousyes & feares as to this perticuler may be removed, I have thought fitt to ordr. & appoint that ye Constable & Overzeers of ye Towne of West Chestr. do give warning to ye said Katherine Harrison to remove out of their prcincts. in some short tyme after notice given, & they are likewise to admonish her to retorne to ye place of her former abode, that they nor their neighbours may receive no furthr. disturbance by her, Given undr. my hand at ffort James in New Yorke this 7th day of July, 1670. Francis Lovelace."

Upon being made aware and notified of her impending fate, Katherine refused to comply, upon which:

The Inhabitants of Westchester making complaint to the Governor, an order was made, August 20, 1670, for her and Captain Ponton to appear before Lovelace at "ffort James in New Yorke" on Wednesday, August 24, when "those of ye Towne that have ought to object agt. them doe like'wise attend, where I shall endeavor a Composure of this difference betweene them." On August 25, the Governor gave his decision in the form of an Order: he recited that several addresses had been made by "Inhabitants of West Chestr. on behalfe of ye rest desiring that" she should be ordered to remove "and not permitted to stay wthin. their jurisdiction upon an apprehension they have of her grounded upon some troubles she hath layne undr. at Wethersfeild upon suspition of Witchcraft."

Unfortunately, her reputation created from her experiences in Connecticut had riled her new neighbors here in New York.

We know from George Lincoln Burr's research and "from Mr. Paltsits, printed by him with especial care and with valuable notes, in the Minutes of the Executive Council of New York (Albany, 1910), 1. 390-395, Il. 52-55. The originals of the documents perished in the fire which befell the State Capitol at Albany on March 29, 1911; the Harrison documents were but slightly damaged."

It was then decided by the magistrate:

The reasons for this suspicion do not so clearly appear to me; yet notwithstanding, to give as much satisfaction as may be to the complainants who pretend their fears to be of a public concern, I have not thought absolutely to determine the matter at present, but do suspend it until the next General Court of Assizes. In the case of Katherine Harrison, widow, who was bound to the good behavior upon complaint of some of the inhabitants of Weschester until the holding of this court: It is ordered that, in regard there is nothing that appears against her deserving the continuance of that obligation, she is to be released from it, and hath liberty to remain in the town of Westchester where she now resides, or anywhere else in the government of New York during her pleasure.

In October 1670 Katherine Harrison's vindication became known to all.

ELIZABETH GARLICK, THE EASTHAMPTON WITCH

Marie Williams wrote in the *New York Almanack* of Elizabeth Garlick's situation:

The 1650s was not an easy time to be a woman, especially if a neighbor held a personal grudge. In East Hampton, Long Island in 1657 Elizabeth "Goody" Garlick was accused of witchcraft, after 16-year-old Elizabeth Gardiner Howell became ill and suffered fevered dreams and delusions.

It was alleged that Garlick was seen dressed in black standing at the foot of her sick bed before she passed away. One of the tell-tale signs of witchcraft was said to be the appearance of a witch in dreams. The town justices held hearings for three weeks taking thirteen witness depositions against Elizabeth Garlick.

Important to remember is that this situation happened thirty-five years before the Salem witch trials; today's Easthampton was known then as East Hampton. The trouble began in February 1658, when the sixteen-year-old Elizabeth Gardiner Howell, recently having given birth to a child, became very sick. The story goes that she screamed, "A witch! A witch! Now you are come to torture me because I spoke two or three words against you!" Her family was summoned, including her prominent local figure of a father, Lion Gardiner, a former military officer.

Her father asked what she was referring to, what did she see, to which she replied, "A black thing at the bed's feet." The following day, Howell died, having already named and blamed Elizabeth Garlick, who, unfortunately for her, was a local resident who often quarreled with neighbors. Garlick was blamed for the usual illnesses, disappearances, livestock deaths, injuries to her neighbors, and making children ill.

Elizabeth Howell's mother swore that she was with her daughter when she had her visions. Goodwife Simmons swore that she was there as well and that Elizabeth had told her that Garlick "had pricked her with pins." Eleven other neighbors made many other accusations. Supposedly, Garlick was a witch and had used witchcraft to poison their breastmilk and cause children to become ill or die. She supposedly also had used witchcraft to injure or cause death to neighbors' farm animals.

With so many neighbors making charges against her, judges could see the pattern of one person as a recurring witness mentioned in the majority of accusations—a woman named Goody Davis. Never directly testifying against Garlick, but by influencing so many others, Davis accused Garlick of being a witch. The accusations included causing the death of two children and another to vanish, a man to die, a pig and her piglets to die during birthing, and an ox to break a leg.

Garlick's husband, Joshua, had been employed to work on Lion Gardiner's Long Island estate. Some of Gardiner's surviving correspondence mentions him as a trusted employee. Gardiner had also entrusted Joshua Garlick with carrying large sums of his money to make purchases.

The Garlick case was sent to the Particular Court of Connecticut in Hartford since at the time, Long Island was a part of Connecticut.

John Winthrop the Younger, the new local sheriff, and other local magistrates found Elizabeth Garlick not guilty. Connecticut state historian Walter Woodward, an associate professor at the University of Connecticut, stated that Winthrop "saw witchcraft cases as an incidence of community pathology. The pattern is clear in cases in which he is involved. It's the pattern of not finding the witches quite guilty, but putting pressure on them to better conform to social norms. At the same time, he acknowledges the justification of the community to be concerned about witchcraft, but he never empowers the community to follow through on that."

Gardiner and Winthrop were longtime associates who together had established the settlement of Saybrook, during the

Pequot Wars. The actual trial transcripts do not exist but the court's directive of not guilty does, and further instruction from the court included and made perfectly clear that both the Garlicks and the community of East Hampton take notice: "It is desired and expected by this court that you should carry neighborly and peaceably without just offense, to Jos. Garlick and his wife, and that they should do the like to you."

Even back then there was legal recourse that Elizabeth and Joshua Garlick had at their disposal, and Joshua sued Goody Davis for defamation. The couple then continued to live in East Hampton, while Davis died shortly after Elizabeth's trial. No more accusations of witchcraft occurred afterwards in East Hampton.

A 2012 *Smithsonian Magazine* article states that John Hanc proposed that "Elizabeth Garlick may have been spared by Winthrop who later became governor of the colony. Hanc says Winthrop was a skeptic when it came to magic, the role the devil played in magic, and the ability of ordinary people to practice magic. Winthrop tended to believe accused witches were living violating societal norms, not laws. In the Garlick decision, Winthrop told the townspeople of East Hampton to act neighborly towards one another."

RALPH AND MARY HALL, THE SETAUKET WITCHES

In the case of Ralph and Mary Hall of Setauket (now Brookhaven), Long Island, they were accused of causing the death of their neighbor George Wood and his child by way of witchcraft. At the time, New York law did not recognize witchcraft as a crime, therefore the case was prosecuted as a murder case.

According to the website of the Three Village Historical Society, "The Court of Assizes was composed of the Governor, the Council and the Justices of the Peace in attendance. The Court convened annually in New York City to hear appeals from the inferior courts and to exercise original jurisdiction in serious criminal matters. In later years, it exercised some legislative functions. The tribunal was the court of last resort unless the case was appealable to the Crown in London. The original documents of the Hall trial held before the Court of Assizes, along with many other historical records, perished in the 1911 fire at the State Capital in Albany. The proceedings of the Hall case were recorded in volume IV of *The Documentary History of the State of New-York* published in 1851." You can read the entire contents of the proceedings on the Three Village Historical Society website (tvhs .org) as well as on the website of the Historical Society of the New York Courts (history.nycourts.gov).

Blake Bell, who now resides in North Carolina, was town historian of Pelham, New York, from 2005 through 2020. On his blog, *Historic Pelham*, he sheds light on the plight of Ralph and Mary Hall in chilling detail:

> The witch hunt was underway. George Wood had grown sick, languished, and died. After his death, his widow had a child who also grew sick, languished, and died. Something was terribly wrong in the English settlement of Seatalcott (also known as Setauket) on Long Island (today's Town of Brookhaven). The only explanations for such incomprehensible losses were the "wicked and detestable Arts"

known as "witchcraft and Sorcery." A monumental witch hunt followed.

In 1665, New Yorkers Ralph and Mary Hall found themselves battling for their lives. The pair was accused of using witchcraft and sorcery beginning on Christmas day, 1664 and at various times thereafter to cause the sicknesses and subsequent deaths of George Wood and the new baby of his widow, Ann Rogers. The Constable and Town officials of Seatalcott charged the pair with murder by sorcery and witchcraft. Ralph and Mary Hall were dragged before the first session of the first Court of Assizes for the Colony of New York.

The Court of Assizes for the Colony of New York was established under the Duke's Laws in 1665. The first session of the Court began on September 28, 1665 at New York before the Governor of the Colony, his Council, and the Justices of the Peace of the so-called East Riding of Yorkshire, a judicial district that was "ridden" on horseback by Justices of the Peace to dispense justice and that included Long Island.

Brought before the court, Ralph and Mary pled not guilty, agreeing to be tried by a judge and jury. The verdict is as follows:

The Court there upon, gave this sentence, That the man should bee bound Body and Goods for his wives Apperance, at the next Sessions, and so on from Sessions to Sessions as long as they stay wthin this Government, In the meane while, to bee of their good Behavior. So they were return'd into the Sheriffs Custody, and upon Entring into a Recognizance, according to the Sentence of the Court, they were released.

A Release to Ralph Hall and Mary his wife from the Recognizance they entred into at the Assizes.

These Are to Certify all whom it may Concerne That Ralph Hall and Mary his wife (at present living upon Great Minifords Island) are hereby released and acquitted from any and all Recognizances, bonds of appearance or othr obligations entred into by them or either of them for the peace or good behavior upon account of any accusation or Indictemt upon suspition of Witch Craft brought into the Cort of Assizes against them in the year 1665. There haveving beene no direct proofes nor furthr prosecucion of them or eithr of them since. Given undr my hand at Fort James in New Yorke this 21th day of August 1668.

On August 21, 1668, the release signed at Fort James freed Ralph and Mary Hall. They later fled to the Manor of Pelham in Westchester County, New York.

Blake Bell explains:

It seems likely that Thomas Pell's pangs of remorse over his family's earlier involvement as witnesses at the witchcraft trial of Goody Knapp, who was executed after a finding that she was a witch, led him to allow Ralph and Mary Hall to settle on Great Minneford Island (today's City

Island) that he owned. Indeed, as I have noted before, the Reverend Nathaniel Brewster who began preaching in Setauket the same year Ralph and Mary Hall were accused by local authorities of witchcraft and sorcery was a stepson of Pelham founder Thomas Pell and preached periodically in Eastchester, once part of the Manor of Pelham until Thomas Pell sold the land to the so-called Ten Families who founded the settlement. Brewster may well have played a role in helping Ralph and Mary Hall settle on his stepfather's island.

NEARBY NEW ENGLAND

New England shared all the same deadly circumstances as witch-crazed Europe, including political turmoil, autonomy of local courts, war, and the important stake in trials held by clerical figures. Once these conditions waned, so did the Salem witch trials.

But New York's Reformed Church community actually had a hand in halting Salem's witch trials, through a variety of letters from New York to Massachusetts Governor Phips in 1692. Seemingly, it worked.

One of these letters by Jacob Melyen, originally in Dutch, translated reads:

July 11, 1692 . . . another punishment of God has come among us, there are about 20 or more people in and around Salem, who are as if possessed by the Devil, and are ill with wonderful convulsions and falling and tormented by great and strange pains. And as if they were deprived of their sanity and unable to come to their senses, they accuse many honest people of being sorcerers and witches, naming 3 or 4 ministers and one of them lies in irons, and some 200 have been accused and most of them thrown into prison. Mr. Willard was also named by these ridiculous people; Captain Alden and many decent people have been sitting in prison for 2 months already. One has been hung. 6 or 7 of the accused have been condemned to death, to the great sorrow of their friends. Throughout the countryside, the excessive gullibility of the magistrates has caused that which the tormented or possessed people bring in against someone together with other trivial circumstances to be taken as substantially true and convincing testimony against the accused, because the possessed say that they see the shape of those they accuse, and that they torment their people by means of witchcraft, even if their real bodies are far away, and that the shapes bite them, pinch them, stab them with pins, yea inflict 100 strange and wondrous torments, that [I] fear too much is believed, the Lord wants to provide for, and maintain each in the true belief in God, in opposition to the devils and their devilish artificers, whose work it is whenever possible to seduce god's elect.

Sir, I do not doubt that you have read many histories of devilish proceedings, and may well have a pamphlet that points out and refutes in a godly way these superstitions and mistakes, that you could send to me for my own satisfaction and instruction, for in my opinion it goes against the Rule of God's word, that a person can broker a contract with the Devil, the hellish enemy as it is called, and extend his chains so that they bring about at will the deaths of other innocent people, old and young, babies and the unborn, and overthrow the whole rule of God's divine providence. Whatever service you would be pleased to do me in loaning a book when next you write shall be gratefully acknowledged and the book will be carefully returned. I have asked Mr. Mather for something special and worth reading, but have not yet obtained anything that can be sent, great wonders are to be expected at the end of the play such as the pen cannot trust, the more as Dudley claims to have copies of my letters, be it from Helcot the Quaker, or Adolfs people through Koner, or by what Devil's art or instrument I know not. On top of this, on the fifth of July 1692 some 14 or 16 houses, shops and warehouses burned on the north side of Boston, near the waterside from Major Clark's red brick wall and on to the next street, not far from Mr. Milborns.

—Your servant and friend, Jacob Melijn

THE WITCH OF SALEM, NEW YORK

Marie Williams, writing for the *New York Almanack*, tells of another witchcraft trial in upper New York: "In the midst of the American Revolution, in the town of Salem (now near the New York–Vermont border in Washington County, NY), there was another witch trial, of a sort. Salem, NY, much like Salem, MA, has a very religious past."

This early upstate New York community was founded by Presbyterian Reverend Dr. Thomas Clark, having emigrated from Ireland in the mid-1760s with his congregation. Dr. Clark's congregation first settled in nearby Stillwater, on the Hudson River, then settled in what is now Salem, New York. They were able to purchase a portion of a tract of 25,000 acres. A settlement had already been established, with many New England settlers already there. Margaret and George Telford were accused of witchcraft in 1777.

Local historians documented tensions between George Telford and his neighbors for varying spiritual beliefs; he was a devout Presbyterian, which frequently led to clashes with neighbors. A strict observer of the Sabbath, unlike his neighbors, he complained of his neighbors to local authorities with little resolution.

Furthermore, writes Marie Williams, "In the summer and fall of 1777, the villagers found themselves in the path of General John Burgoyne's Saratoga Campaign. Some villagers, including the Telfords, found refuge at Burgoyne's camp in Fort Edward, but as a consequence were branded Loyalists. At the same time, while in Burgoyne's camp, the Telfords were considered disloyal to the Crown and forced to pay for shelter (a British soldier who knew the family paid part of the cost)."

Neighbor upon neighbor, the accusations started that Margaret Telford was most likely the cause of a dairy problem. Presiding over the ensuing trial was Reverend Dr. Clark, with accusers and accused being members of his church. Fortunately, many of the congregation testified on record that Margaret was an "upstanding citizen of the village and was a good Christian woman."

Dr. Clark then examined all the evidence presented and determined there was not nearly enough evidence against Margaret to try her as a witch. However, being found lacking to be a witch didn't always prevent the accused from being ostracized by the community, neighbors against neighbors.

Although the end result was largely positive, it must have been uncomfortable going forward in such a community, but according to local historians, Margaret and George Telford remained in good standing with the Salem Presbyterian congregation throughout the rest of their lives.

John R. Henderson, retired social sciences librarian at Ithaca College, whose great-grandmother's great-grandmother was Margaret Telford, provides more information from his research:

Salem, New York, located north of Albany between the Hudson River and the Vermont border, is not known as the home of witches or witch trials. But a witch trial, of a sort, was indeed held there in 1777, more than eighty years after the more famous (or infamous) witch trials of Salem, Massachusetts. . . .

The Rev. Dr. Thomas Clark played a crucial role in the witch investigation. To set the stage, let me tell you a bit about him. He was a remarkable individual who in several ways was unique among Presbyterian ministers who came to America. Born in Scotland in 1720, he was educated at the University of Glasgow, first earning a degree as Doctor of Medicine in 1744 and then completing his ministerial studies in 1748. In between degrees Clark served a soldier who battled against Bonny Prince Charlie (1745–46).

Reverend Clark's wife and child died in the early 1760s, which may have led to him coming to America. As reported in the *New York Gazette*, August 6, 1764: "Last week in the Ship John, from Newry, Ireland, Luke Kiersted, master, there arrived about three hundred passengers, a hundred and forty of whom, together with the Rev. Clarke, embarked on the 30th ult., with their stores, farming and manufacturing utensils, in two sloops, for Albany, from whence they are to proceed to the lands near Lake George, which were lately surveyed for their accommodation, as their principal view is to carry on the linen and hempen manufacture to which they were all brought up."

Upon arriving in America in the spring of 1765, Reverend Clark bought half of a 25,000-acre tract of land in Salem, New York.

"The accused witch of Salem, New York, was a member of Clark's congregation named Margaret Tilford," wrote John Henderson. "She and her husband George were not among the original members of Clark's congregation, so to a certain extent they might have been viewed as outsiders. There are some unanswerable questions about her name, both first and last. Although her name was Margaret, in Robert Blake's account of the witch accusation, he calls her Betty. Perhaps she was known as Betty; or perhaps Robert Blake, telling the story seventy years later, confused the names of the mother and her daughter, Elizabeth or, as is common in our family, mis-spoke the one thinking the other. To the befuddlement of genealogists, their surname is spelled both 'Telford' and 'Tilford' in various documents, and both Tilfords and Telfords are found among their descendants."

The couple joined the congregation seven years after it was founded, both having been born in Scotland. They had arrived in New York City and traveled up the Hudson River, having to bury their infant son along the way, one of their five children. The family arrived in what is now Salem in August of 1772.

According to Henderson, "George Telford was extremely dutiful in following his faith and, as not unusual for a Presbyterian, a strict Sabbatarian. For example, one Saturday, late in the day, he took his grain to the mill to be ground. The miller told him there would be a long wait and suggested he leave it to pick up later. George left his grain and went home. The next day, being the Sabbath, George drove his family in his wagon and passed the mill to church. While George was at church, the miller must have recognized the wagon and decided to do George a favor by placing the ground grist into the Telford wagon. George didn't discover it until he was home. Scrupulous in observing the Sabbath day, George took the grist back to the miller the first thing Monday morning. Knowing that hauling the grist home, even if he had done it unknowingly, was a violation of the fourth commandment, George Telford wanted no part of the Sabbath-violating grist."

On his way to church one Sunday, George noticed a neighbor with an ax splitting wood; to him it was a clear violation of the Sabbath. George then reported the incident to the local magistrate only to have the matter dropped, but some lingering tensions between the two may have then set off a chain of events.

Then the Revolutionary War started, increasing the types of tensions that in many communities contributed to the witchcraft hysteria.

I have written about the events that unfolded next in *Haunted Catskills* (2013) and *Images of America: Kinderhook* (2019) and was pleased to come across new information from John Henderson: "The settlements around present-day Salem lay near the path of Gentleman Johnny Burgoyne's march from Canada to Saratoga, and in the summer of 1777, the area was the scene of a war atrocity. An Iroquois scouting party led by a chief called Le Loup (the wolf) was allied to Burgoyne. After claiming some injury, Le Loup vowed revenge on the town. In Argyle, the Allen family was attacked in their home, and seven people, including women, children, and slaves, were killed. In another incident, near Fort Edward, Jane McCrea was attacked and killed."

Burgoyne's Fort Edward camp being the only safe place to flee to, the Telfords and many of their neighbors fled there, only to be branded as traitors later on. "The following year, on April 17, 1778, George Telford, William Blake, and two other men were summoned before the Albany County Board of Commissioners for Detecting and Defeating Conspiracies 'for going to the Enemy,'" shared Henderson.

Captain John McKellop posted their bail, defended their motives, and spoke up on their behalf, explaining that the need for safety and fear of being scalped would have prompted anyone to flee to this stronghold. Freed and allowed to return home, they were subjected to "their entering into Recognizance with security for their future good behavior as good and faithful Subjects and monthly appearance before any one of the Commissioners."

"It was the same year (I think) in which Burgoyne's invasion took place, that a most foolish and deplorable superstition took place," Salem native and eyewitness Robert Blake stated on November 5, 1847.

Besides being branded traitors, the Telfords then had to deal with neighbors accusing them of witchcraft, including, ironically, one who advised another neighbor using a divination tool of cards and forecasting/fortune-telling. Neighbor Archy Livinston had cows whose milk was not churning for butter, and demanded to know who was responsible for his misfortune. The card reader gave a description of who had "bewitched" the cream, and apparently the only woman who fit this description was Margaret Telford. Once Livingston publicly stated the accusation, the consequences started to befall the Telfords in various uncomfortable ways.

When the local magistrate refused to get involved, and Presbyterians were cognizant of separating church and state, it was decided that the church would be the authority to settle the matter, and both Livingston and the Telfords were members of Reverend Clark's church. A witchcraft trial was not held, but an investigation was carried out by Clark. Luckily for the Telfords, many congregants testified to Margaret's character. When the card reader and his fortune-telling methods were investigated, the matter was dropped since it was decided that there was "nothing tangible here for the church to take hold of," meaning that Margaret could be cleared of the accusations. But since Reverend Clark would soon leave the area for South Carolina, and at the time of his death there still had been no formal ruling in regards to Margaret, the matter was never officially closed.

Among neighbors, ill will and superstition does not evaporate overnight, and in some cases never does. The Telfords had to endure long-term consequences of Margaret being accused of being a witch; they and their adult children were shunned and excluded from many of life's happy events in the community. Staying in the community and rising above the difficulties, the Telfords lived out their days there, both being buried in Salem's cemetery.

We have this valuable information of a lost time from John Henderson as a descendant:

> I first learned about the witch of Salem, NY, from Robert Cree Duncan. He credits Ernest H. Tilford for uncovering the story and communicating the details of it to him sometime in the early 1960s. Ernest Tilford praises Asa Fitch in a letter to the New York Historical Association's journal for showing "1) from what part of Scotland and when my father's ancestors came, 2) who comprised the family and with what neighbors they migrated, 3) that they first settled in Fitch's Point, 4) that in 1777 the wife of the emigrant was accused of witchcraft and 5) the strict sabbatarianism of these Scottish people." Fitch's source, in 1847, was Robert Blake, then aged 85 years old. Blake had

The Salem Revolutionary Cemetery. The three flat ground stones from left to right are engraved with the following: "George Tilford, died July 23, 1813, age 85 yrs." "Margaret Tilford, wife of George Tilford, died Sept. 15, 1807, age 76 yrs." "James Tilford, Departed this life by a fall from his wagon. Dec. 15, 1808 in the 42d year of his age." The epitaph on Margaret's stone reads "Hear what the voice of heaven proclaims, for all the Pious dead. Sweet is the savour of their names and soft their dying bed." Courtesy of Al Cormier, Salem Town Historian

come over with his family and the Telfords when he and one of the Telford boys, John, were 10 years old. He would have been about 15 years old when the witch accusation was made. I have only seen excerpts of Blake's account as they were transcribed in Bob Duncan's "The Telford Family" chapter in Joseph R. Henderson and Robert Cree Duncan's privately printed Henderson Family History, 1986. Blake's account was originally recorded in Asa Fitch in 1847 as part of his historical and genealogical master-work "Notes for a History of Washington County, New

York." The account was published in an article in volume 73 of the New York Genealogical and Biographical Record (1942). Bob Duncan's transcription has been corroborated by the Fitch Gazetteer of Washington County, New York by Kenneth A. Perry (1999), which summarizes the story that originally appeared in article 59 of Fitch's unfinished seven volume manuscript history.

An earlier version of this story also appeared in August 21 and 28, 1998, issues of the Salem Press. Thanks to Al Cormier, Salem Town Historian for showing an interest in the tale and making the arrangements for having it published in the paper. Ernest H. Tilford saw the article in the paper and sent a letter to the editor concerning it. The letter was published September 17, 1998, and I have reproduced on this Web site with permission of the author, who was given permission by the Salem Press. Since my essay appeared in the *Salem Press*, I have had exchanged several letters with my new-found many-times-removed cousin. My thanks to him for his suggestions and criticism. They have been invaluable in helping me improve upon the story.

NEW YORK'S LAST WITCHCRAFT TRIAL: NAUT KANNIF

In 1816, New York saw its last witchcraft trial. Jane "Naut" Kannif settled in Clarksville, New York, now known as the hamlet of West Nyack. She lived from the late 1700s to the mid-1800s and was the wife and then widow of a Scottish physician. So in a small town she apparently checked off all the boxes for being a witch in the eyes of the narrow-minded: she was a widow and newcomer, she sported colorful hair and clothing, she had a black cat and a talking parrot, and she mostly kept to herself in a village where everyone knew one another (and probably knew everyone else's business too). Like Hulda, Jane Kannif was known to harvest local herbs to help people.

Working with herbs and perhaps casting spells, if the local farmers had their way, they would have bound her hands and feet, attached a heavy metal of some sort, and thrown her into the pond near what is now Demarest Mill Road. Sinking meant you were innocent of being a witch, although perhaps now dead. Floating would have meant a death sentence too, for surely then one was a witch, doomed to be burned at the stake or hanged. Due to the farming misfortunes that commonly occurred at the time such as butter not churning and cows failing to produce milk, the farmers wanted someone to blame.

By the 1800s, most witchcraft trials in America had ended and had long been thought to be barbaric, unnecessary, and uncivilized, but there was this one left to play out. Also by this time, local judges would have dismissed out of hand accusations of witchcraft, so in this case, the township took it upon themselves to try Jane. When a neighbor complained of a pins-and-needles-type pain, villagers went to Jane's house where they allegedly found her to have a doll with pins sticking out—a voodoo doll if you like—and so were convinced that she was the cause of the neighbor's pain, as well as being a witch.

Jane was spared the dunking test, however, and a different test was utilized. A scale was used to weigh her against a brass-bound Dutch Bible. If she was lighter, it meant she was a witch;

if she was heavier, it meant she was not a witch. Naturally, Kannif passed the test and avoided execution.

"Kanniff's story had a happy ending, but most witch trials did not. Between the 15th and 18th centuries, an estimated 50,000 women were killed for witchcraft in Europe and America. Since there's no such thing as actual supernatural witchcraft, most of those women were just as innocent as Jane 'Naut' Kanniff. Women who fell victim to witch-hunts were targeted due to a combination of sexism and religious superstition. When something bad happens, it's human nature to look to blame someone else or the supernatural rather than admit it was your own fault or no one's fault and just bad luck," states T. Z. Barry on his blog (tzbarry.com).

"That the Clarkstown incident happened can not be doubted. The other two instances mentioned were actual court cases. Neither of the versions of what happened in Clarkstown show that the session in Auert Polhemus' grist mill (or was it Pye's fulling mill?) was anything more than a mock trial. To be utterly fair, the 'trial' of Clarkstown's 'witch' should at least be referred to in quotation marks. Dr. Frank R Green, a newspaper man as well as a physician, heard the county's tales from his patients as he made his rounds, and he published a Rockland County history in 1886. The yarn about Naut Kannif was still fresh enough in his time so he could have heard it from an eye-witness, or one inclined to boast that his father had tried a witch. In his version, there is nothing about threatening to throw Mrs. Kannif into the mill pond. That was added when Justice Arthur S. Tompkins' history was published in

1902." (Quoted from R.C., a contributor to Find A Grave, on its memorial page for Jane "Naut" Kannif.)

Linda Zimmermann, a Hudson Valley author and scientist who regularly is featured on Sci-Fi and Travel Channel paranormal television shows, interviewed local historians for information on this colorful character and heard that Jane "stood out like a tartan in a tulip field," being a woman of Scottish descent in the heavily Dutch population of the time. You can listen to an excerpt from the "Haunted History" episode of *Crossroads of Rockland History* originally recorded October 2014, wherein Zimmermann interviews Clare Sheridan about Jane "Naut" Kannif, the Witch of West Nyack, aka the Witch of Clarkstown. Zimmermann lists sources such as the late Rockland County historian John Scott, Frank Bertangue Green, MD, and the Rockland County website to learn more about this fascinating tale.

Dr. Green wrote of the widow Kannif: "Jane, or as she was called in the vernacular of the Clarksville people, Naut Kanniff, seems to have been exceedingly eccentric, a person who would now be regarded by alienists as insane; but her vagaries at the worst took a harmless form. She was odd in dress, preferring parti-colors of wondrous diversity, queer in the fashion of arranging her hair. She was unsocial in a neighborhood where everyone knew each other; and morose or erratic when forced to meet people. With these traits and habits, she combined one other. From her deceased husband she had gathered a smattering of medicine, and now, when placed where she could get at the herbs known in her Materia Medica, she made wondrous decoctions with which she treated such as came to her for aid, and I have been informed by those who knew her, with most excellent results."

A play called *The Clarkstown Witch*, written by Augustus Nowak in the 1950s, was performed several times in Rockland County.

THE WITCH OF ESPERANCE

Near Cobleskill, New York, is the beautiful town of Esperance (the French word for "hope"), a tiny village (population of 345) west of Schenectady, with a sad story from the 1800s. Here, around Halloween of 2017, the New York Folklore Society and the William G. Pomeroy Foundation erected a folklore marker dedicated to the Witch of Esperance.

Some say her name is not known to us, but others say they actually do know who this legend pertains to. The marker reads "French settler accused of witchcraft by New England settlers. Killed by a silver bullet shot through her window." In her case, there wasn't even a witchcraft trial—villagers just took matters into their own hands.

In one of the most ridiculous stories ever of a woman being accused of witchcraft, it's truly scary to learn of the awful things some villagers did to their neighbors in olden times. A widowed Frenchwoman, the Witch of Esperance was accused of being able to use her apron to glide across Schoharie Creek, and then tie it back on with the apron being totally dry when she reached the other side. Of course, she was also blamed for failing crops and dying cattle.

New York church where villagers decided the fate of the Witch of Esperance. Library of Congress

Susan Defeo wrote in October 2007 for the *Cape May County Herald* that:

> I had a gravestone in my driveway. There it stood, Elizabeth Kniskern, wife of John, died 1854. You see, we owned a 15-acre farmette, not to be confused with a 15-acre farm which raises actual animals or crops. The farmette was located on top of a foothill in beautiful Cobleskill, NY, next to the old Kniskern place. Apparently, the farmer plowed the gravesite over for his pumpkin patch and placed the tablet neatly on our side of the fence well before we bought the property. When we sold the acreage, the new owner told us in no uncertain terms to take the gravestone with us.

Legend has it that after her husband died, Elizabeth was left to run the farm with her only child, a son. As he got older, the son wished for a more exciting life and decided he would enlist in the army. In those days the postmaster acted as recruitment officer. Elizabeth marched right down to the village of Esperance and under threat of a town-wide hex, warned the postmaster not to allow her son to sign up. Well, long story short, the son joined up and died during his tour of duty. Elizabeth put Esperance on hex alert and strange things began to happen. First, the post office had a fire. Then locals' wells ran dry, animals fell sick, and barns burned down. What was the town to do? At a solemn conclave in the stone church, her neighbors voted her death. To kill the witch, her executioners fired a silver bullet, melted down from a spoon, and shot her through the window of her cabin. They then buried her upside down, under an evergreen tree, which stands on the north side of the village to this day.

A second version of the story puts Elizabeth as a young French widow with children. Unable to speak English and mingle with the townsfolk, she became the object of suspicion. They shot her through her window as she cooked dinner over an open fire, her little ones playing beside her. Different beginning, same sad end.

Local legend has it that she was buried upside down, with a stake in her head, below a pine tree; its roots keep her there and prevent her from rising and seeking revenge upon villagers.

Many thanks to Preston Gibson of the *Cape May County Herald*, in personal correspondence with me, for providing such a great historical reference, and to Elizabeth Goodermote for bringing this story to my attention.

THE SEVEN SUTHERLAND SISTERS OF CAMBRIA, NIAGARA COUNTY

In *Spirits of the Niagara Wine Trail* (2015), an excerpt of which can also be read on the Facebook page for *Haunted Catskills*, Mason Winfield wrote about the enigmatic upstate New York Sutherland sisters, known for their extremely long and lush hair, who resided on Ridge Road near Warren's Corners in Cambria, Niagara County:

> As if envisioning a stage act all along, the Sutherland family never trimmed their seven daughters, in birth-order Sarah, Victoria, Isabella, Grace, Naomi, Dora, and Mary. They even concocted some kind of snake-oil treatment suspected of helping the hair, which Mrs. Sutherland slathered on the girls' heads every morning before they went to school. Skanky hair couldn't have been unique in the age, but the Sutherlands' doctored locks gave off an effluvium their schoolfellows found objectionable. (In later years the family would mass produce and distribute something called "The Seven Sutherland Sisters' Hair Fertilizer," and the name was said to be suggestive of the smell.) By 1884 the family enterprise included production and sales through a New York company of "The 7 Sutherland Sisters Hair Growe." But the

Miss Grace Sutherland, 1890. Wikimedia Commons, George Eastman House Collection

product was in fact fake, being made of witch hazel and bay rum with traces of hydrochloric acid, salt, and magnesium.

In the late 1870s, the girls with their family became a singing act touring with P. T. Barnum, according to Mason. The sisters were sometimes accosted by fans with scissors, who tried to get snips of their hair. Sarah, Victoria, Isabella, Grace, Naomi, Dora, and Mary lived in a mansion in Warner's Corners, New York, and may have been the subject of gossip and jealousy, so were talked about as dabbling in witchcraft and Spiritualism.

"This could refer to fits of insanity, but it might allude to Mary's practice of launching curses at those who displeased her," Mason writes, part of why the Sutherland sisters were gossiped about as being witches. When their parents died, the sisters became among the wealthiest people in America from what they inherited. They were extremely famous in their time, much like big celebrities today, but their stories didn't end well. Mismanagement of their wealth led them back to poverty, and several deaths occurred, including suicide. In 1926 one of the sisters, Dora, was hit and killed by a car in California while there in hopes of having a movie made of their life story. "She was cremated in Hollywood, but Mary and Grace had no money to pay for the services, so (at the date of this article) Dora's ashes are still in Hollywood, awaiting claimants," reported *Yankee Magazine* in the April 1982 article "The Amazing Seven Sutherland Sisters and Their 'Niagara of Curls.'"

THE WONDERFUL WIZARD OF OZ
AND L. FRANK BAUM

Many of us remember the first time we saw the movie *The Wizard of Oz* featuring a frog-green witch and how that affected us. A truly terrifying icon, not forgotten in modern times, this witch was created by author L. Frank Baum, who for a time lived in Syracuse. The 1939 film was made forty years after the book's publication.

Baum lived from 1856 until 1919, and in 1899 his children's poetry collection *Gooseman* was a national best-seller. Some of the controversy that has surrounded the Oz book includes a 1989 Tennessee lawsuit, when seven Fundamentalist Christian families filed suit hoping to get the book banned from public schools due to their disapproval of how the novel portrayed nice witches. Glinda the Good Witch can be seen to represent the mother archetype in her role as always helping and guiding.

Fred R. Hamlin's musical extravaganza, *The Wizard of Oz.* U.S. Lithograph Co., 1903; Library of Congress

If "The Legend of Sleepy Hollow" is considered America's first published ghost story, then *The Wonderful Wizard of Oz* can be considered America's first published fairy tale. Some parts of this tale may have been inspired by the author's feisty suffragist mother-in-law who devoted her life to the empowerment of women and also spoke out against slavery; her Fayetteville, New York, home was actually a part of the Underground Railroad.

The Wonderful Wizard of Oz has been theorized to have several hidden meanings pertaining to American politics, such as the Wizard representing the US president, having little or no real power himself. The book's dominant theme, however, is that of self-sufficiency and resilience. In the book and film, Dorothy's ruby slippers, stolen from the Wicked Witch, represent a symbol of revolution and are a tool to liberate the oppressed.

Pam Grossman wrote in her book *Waking the Witch* (2019) of *The Wonderful Wizard of Oz* that "it forever stamped the concept of good witches and bad witches into popular consciousness." Baum's book was incredibly ahead of its time. In 1893, Baum's mother-in-law had written about current conditions in regards to how women were treated, believing it to be comparable to the Burning Times. "She believed that witches of Western Europe were persecuted because their wisdom was a threat to the patriarchal church," states Pam, who feels that if not for Baum's mother-in-law, he may have never created the good witch characters. The introduction of the concept of good witches subsequently created many iconic twentieth-century characters in art, books, television, and film. It's one of the ways in which the view of witches has changed from bad to beautiful.

Interestingly, according to Dracula's House of Halloween's Facebook page, originally there was an idea for the movie to "have the Wicked Witch portrayed as a slinky, glamorous villainess in a black sequined costume, inspired by the Wicked Queen in Walt Disney's *Snow White*. Gale Sondergaard was originally cast as the witch in *Oz* and was photographed for two wardrobe tests. One was as a glamorous wicked witch, and another as a conventionally ugly wicked witch. After the decision was made to have an ugly wicked witch, Sondergaard, reluctant to wear the disfiguring makeup and fearing it could damage her career, withdrew from the role."

For Margaret Hamilton, the actress who portrayed the Wicked Witch of the West in the movie, her role was so well played that for the remainder of her life she tried to escape from the creation of her scary character. She did television shows such as *Sesame Street* and *Mr. Roger's Neighborhood*, hoping to be less scary to children and encourage them in the pretend and self-empowerment. Many of us are old enough to remember her appearing on these shows, and while it personally wasn't upsetting to me in any way, I do remember the *Sesame Street* episode making children I knew fearful all over again. From what I understand, it also affected many other children enough that the episode was aired only once. It's hard for us to imagine how Hamilton was genuinely baffled at how scary her movie character was to children everywhere and for decades to come.

Margaret Hamilton as the Wicked Witch of the West in *The Wizard of Oz*, 1939. Photograph by Virgil Apger

PRACTICAL MAGIC

The 1995 novel *Practical Magic* by Alice Hoffman is vastly different from the October 1998 cult classic movie that sprang from it. Directed by Griffin Dunne, the movie employed an actual witch to serve as a consultant to the film. While Dunne felt that she had been properly compensated for her part, she apparently later demanded more money and a portion of the film's proceeds, and threatened to curse everyone associated with the film if her demands weren't met. She eventually got her way when even the film's lawyers were frightened of her and gave in to her monetary demands.

The house featured in the film was so beautiful that reportedly Barbra Streisand wanted to buy it. The movie's producer, Denise Di Novi, chose the book for film adaptation because "witches were exciting, with their powers and magic, and the book presented them in a believable, practical way."

This is a book, a film, and a house that many of us still wish we could live in . . .

The film came out at an auspicious time, with *Charmed* and other witchcraft television shows being aired, and is considered to have been a turning point for witchcraft being accepted in popular culture. And with such beautiful actresses featured in the film, Sandra Bullock and Nicole Kidman, with their long flowing hair and striking fashion, it was a success in terms of changing the perception of witches from bad to beautiful.

In the story, witch sisters Sally and Gillian go to live with witch aunts Frances and Jet after their parents pass away; they are all descended from Maria Owens, who in 1620 passes down a family curse to protect future generations from love—all men unfortunate to love an Owens woman are bound for an early untimely death. Perhaps some consider love itself to be a curse, and Maria, after being spurned by her lover and carrying his child, isolates forever, building a beautiful house using twelve carpenters. She is determined that no one in her family ever feel the pain of love that she has.

Aunts Frances and Jet, Sally, and Gillian all live in the house Maria built on an island off the coast of Massachusetts. Sally swears off magic, except for practical uses, having seen the lengths that some women go to for love by engaging the magic of her aunts. Sister Gillian, who embraces love and magic, and who is continually in trouble, sets off a chain of events so beautifully and humorously played out in the movie.

One major difference between the novel and movie is that after Sally's husband dies, she and her daughters move to Long Island, and Sally buys a house and takes a job at the school attended by her daughters. It's at this Long Island location that she meets Tucson detective Gary Hallet, who is searching for Gillian's missing boyfriend. Hallet is the result of a childhood spell cast by Sally, which she starts to figure out, leading her to start to avoid him, but the chemistry and magic between them is undeniable.

A beautiful book and movie that never gets old.

THE RULES OF MAGIC

When many of those set to be tried escaped from New England in search of a more tolerant place, they found it in Manhattan. While the anti-witchcraft mania raged in New England, spurred by politics, greed and religion, two witch trials had taken place, in 1658 and 1665, one in Queens, the other on Long Island, then called Yorkshire, in the town of Setauket.

—*Excerpt from* The Rules of Magic

The Rules of Magic, Alice Hoffman's 2017 prequel to *Practical Magic*, starts by reminding us that Maria Owens comes to

Massachusetts in 1680 as an enigma. Who fathered her child and how she built the magnificent house using twelve carpenters is a mystery to villagers, but readers will find the answers to those questions in the novel.

This is the story of aunts Frances and Jet and their brother Vincent—the only boy ever born in the Owens family. Vincent honed his magical talents from an early age, with Frances and Jet wanting to learn how to do what he could do. Growing up in New York City in the 1950s, the three Owens children were shunned at school and blamed for any bad luck that befell upon their classmates (as witches commonly are). But the 1960s held a hopeful promise that change was coming.

The children weren't interested in normal school or after-school activities. They were interested in the occult—occult books and making their way to the forbidden Greenwich Village occult shop.

Their mother, Susanna, does not tell them anything of their family or ancestors and wants a normal life for them. The children are invited to spend the summer with Aunt Isabelle in Massachusetts at the house Maria built. They notice immediately on Magnolia Street nearing Maria's house that they will be shunned in Massachusetts just like they were in New York City. Aunt Isabelle receives secret visitors at night seeking out her magic remedies, and during their summer visit the children learn that they are witches and descended from witches.

Frances spends time at the local library, where Maria Owens's diary is kept under lock and key. The diary also contains spells and curses. Frances learns of Maria's despair in unrequited love, and her curse that misfortune will come to any man who falls in love with an Owens woman. Fragrant and colorful, *The Rules of Magic*, even more so than *Practical Magic*, deals with loss. It plays out against some of the significant events in New York City of the 1960s, such as the Stonewall riots.

An ye harm none, do as thou will.

ROSEMARY'S BABY

Published in 1967, Ira Levin's *Rosemary's Baby* is a novel remarkably still in print. The folk horror genre exploded from the 1950s to 1970s. The novel sold very well upon its release, as witchcraft had become a popular topic at the time, and the author's appearance on the *Today Show* certainly fueled interest in the novel. It was one of the books at the time that set off a horror craze that lasted decades.

The Satanic Panic had also set in, setting the stage for Levin to craft a brilliant story about a seemingly normal couple with a seemingly normal pregnancy living in New York City. But the baby would be Satan's child, and in the novel, Levin chooses the date of the baby's birth to be June 25, inverse or opposite of the date of Christ's birth. The novel is very easy to read, and feels real right from the start; having seen the movie first, I knew much of what to expect from the story. And readers will appreciate how faithful to the novel Roman Polanski was in writing the screenplay for the film.

The *New York Times* praised the novel, stating, "Suspense is beautifully intertwined with everyday incidents; the delicate line between belief and disbelief is faultlessly drawn." Truman

Capote opined that it "induces the reader to believe the unbelievable. I believed it and was altogether enthralled." The editor of *Cosmopolitan* magazine, Helen Gurley Brown, said, "A modern classic is a book that people will still want to read one or two hundred years from now. I think *Rosemary Baby* is a good example."

The couple, Rosemary and Guy, are warned by their longtime friend Hutch not to move into their new apartment building due to its creepy history of bizarre recurring deaths and rumors of witchcraft. In the film version of the novel, the exterior shots of the apartment building is The Dakota, reputed to be haunted. The first time the couple has dinner with their new neighbors Roman and Minnie Castevet at their apartment, there is foreshadowing of the Castevets' serious disdain for religion and of the Pope's upcoming visit to New York City.

After what Rosemary thinks is a bad dream in which she is copulating with a creature instead of her husband (she is, in fact, being raped by Satan after being drugged upon eating the chocolate mousse concoction brought over by Minnie), she decides she needs to get away for a week, to leave the city and head upstate to Brewster to friend Hutch's weekend cabin. She returns to her New York City apartment to find that she is pregnant. The Castevets take an unusual interest in her pregnancy, as well as being the first people her husband wants to know of the joyous news. Rosemary is given a charm necklace by Mrs. Castevet containing the pungent-smelling "tannis root."

As Rosemary gets sicker and more gaunt looking, Hutch starts noticing strange things, and when he wants Rosemary to meet him privately to give her a book he's been reading, he doesn't show up due to suddenly falling ill and into a coma. Upon his death, Rosemary is given the book that Hutch was reading, *All of Them Witches*, and starts to figure it all out . . .

In the book, she learns, "In their rituals, they often use the fungus called Devil's Pepper. This is a spongy matter derived from swampy regions having a strong pungent odour. Devil's Pepper is considered to have special powers. It has been used in rituals and worn on charms." Could this be the "tannis" in her necklace?

Her husband's acting career may have suddenly flourished because of his promising their child to the witches and Satanic cult down the hall . . .

People falling ill, committing suicide, and dying may be due to the witches and Satanic cult down the hall . . .

In the novel, Rosemary, like many people at the time and even today, didn't realize that witches are real. In modern times, as witch hysteria waned and witchcraft trials ceased to occur, people came to think of witches as only existing in books and as Halloween costumes.

The 1968 film was both written and directed by Roman Polanski, earned two Oscar nominations, was widely praised by film critics, and was deemed in 2014 worthy of preservation in the National Film Registry by the Library of Congress as being "culturally, historically, or aesthetically significant."

Mia Farrow, who also sings the film's intro song, played the part of Rosemary; other actresses considered were Patty Duke and Goldie Hawn. John Cassavetes played her husband, after the part was turned down by Robert Redford and Jack Nicholson.

"Polanski's film put a Satanic cult right beyond our bedroom walls. Hollywood bled into reality when people read that the Bucklands were practicing Wicca in a basement of a ranch house in Long Island. Most Americans wouldn't discriminate between the real god-and-goddess, nature-based Wicca and Polanski's Hollywood 'Hail Satan!' coven in Manhattan. All they knew was that witches now looked like insurance secretaries or elevator operators, that there were more of them than anyone ever imagined. As Dr. Raymond Buckland told a reporter when asked just how many covens there were in America in 1972, 'It's probably closer to 2000 than 20,'" wrote author Lesley Pratt Bannatyne on her website iskullhalloween.com.

Ira Levin's estate still maintains his website, iralevin.org, where viewers are treated to images of the author's Connecticut home, his writing process, typewritten and handwritten notes, character creation, and inspiration for the novel. There are photographs of letters the author received from readers who both were delighted by and despised the book as well as the author's explanation of how he chose to end the story.

BELL, BOOK AND CANDLE

This beautiful 1958 movie is about Christmastime in New York City and how Gillian, played by Kim Novak, bewitches her upstairs neighbor Shepherd Henderson, played by James Stewart. After Henderson takes his fiancée to the Zodiak jazz club and socializes with Gillian, her brother, and her aunt,

Gillian tells her aunt that she longs for a normal life, and on Christmas Eve sets her sights on her neighbor. She works a spell using her familiar, her cat Pyewacket, and instead of marrying his fiancée on Christmas Day upstate, Henderson falls head over heels for her. (Novak used her own cat for the film, and they were both featured on the cover of *Life* magazine in November 1958.)

Gillian promises to set up a meeting between Henderson, who is a publisher, and the author of a book called *Magic in Mexico*. The author visits Henderson in his office and they discuss the author's next book project, to be called *Magic in Manhattan*, a book of witches in New York City. It's during this meeting that the author tells the publisher that the witches' headquarters is the Zodiac Club, and that male witches are called warlocks.

The trouble begins when Gillian's brother Nicky, played by Jack Lemmon, starts to collaborate with the author, giving him too much witch information, which doesn't sit well with Gillian. When Henderson rejects the manuscript, Gillian decides to tell him what she is.

In this film, witches can't cry or love, and if a witch should fall in love, she would cease to have powers, cease to be a witch, and become human. As mentioned in the movie, "When doing love potions and spells, shake well but don't tell."

What Witches Were Thought to Be, What Witches Really Are

Witches are outsiders, and those among us who have been bullied and ostracized can relate to their plight. These are women who don't need to be rescued by a prince or a king but instead can save themselves.

—*Alice Hoffman,* Practical Magic

oday's witches are taking their power back. They no longer live in fear or have to hide who they are the way they might have done in ancient times. They're entrepreneurs, authors, artists, creators, business owners. Today's modern practitioners of witchcraft and paganism have made great strides since even just the 1970s, the Satanic Panic, and the discrimination of those times, while creating a more accepting landscape for themselves.

Throughout history, male practitioners of witchcraft have identified as witches, with the term *warlock* having the negative connotation of "deceiver" or "trickster." The term is believed to have originated in the fourteenth century, although some sources date it back to AD 1000. In modern Craft practices, *warlock* is considered insulting and derogatory. The term was believed to have been used in ancient Scotland to mean demon, wizard or magician, sorcerer, or practitioner of black magic; it was used to describe male witches but is rarely used by male witches themselves today. In Old English, the *warlock* may have been a translation of a Saxon word and meant oath breaker, traitor, liar, enemy, or devil. It's a term that has also been used for witches who betray their coven/other witches.

To quote R. J. Schwartz, pagan historian, "The worst part is that the crimes of the past are still embedded in the world we live in today."

Author RuneWolf, in a 2004 essay for Witchvox, wrote that he recently began to refer to himself as a warlock: "We are told by many modern Witches, particularly those involved with the various flavors of Feminist Wicca and Witchcraft, that we are reclaiming the power and positive meaning of the word 'Witch' after centuries of patriarchal oppression and denigration. Cool—I am completely down with that. So why not do the same for 'Warlock'?"

Some modern-day male witches are reclaiming the term *warlock* to differentiate between the masculine and the feminine. In the 1960s television sitcom *Bewitched*, warlocks were humorously portrayed, in another example of poetic license and the media's take on an ancient subject. In modern times, *warlock* has often been misinterpreted to be synonymous with words like fortune-teller, soothsayer, astrologer, clairvoyant, conjurer, magician, medium, necromancer, juggler, mage, wizard, shaman, witch doctor, alchemist, and prophet. In modern times, too, people have tended to think *witch* meant female while *warlock* meant male—a sort of assigning gender to these terms—which is erroneous.

Think of a plumber, electrician, or doctor as meaning either male or female, such is the witch.

"An ye harm none, do what ye will," stated in various forms, is a moral guide and mantra that has been in place for some time and illustrates the kindness towards others that has always been part and parcel of the witch's craft.

To the religious and superstitious, witches, warlocks, and witchcraft were considered treason against God, with male and female witches cavorting and fornicating with the Devil. Witches supposedly engaged in animal and human sacrifice, causing storms, poor crops, and illness, and were blamed for misfortunes of any kind really. In many religions, using the Devil as a cause of evil and wrongdoing contrasts with the witch's belief that the individual is always accountable, and that evil is largely man-made.

Darrell Pinckney of the Caretakers of History project, Albany, explained it in this way in personal correspondence to me:

Witchcraft is a broad term as you already know. I can say that generally speaking, Witchcraft itself is a methodology or a skill. It is a way of working with energy to produce a result. Wicca, however, teaches a spiritual philosophy and has its own code of ethics, concepts, rituals and deities. The general rules or guidance some Wiccans often follow are:

- Do as you will but harm no living thing.
- Everything you do comes back threefold.
- Wiccans are NOT Devil worshipers. Satan is a Christian creation. The horned God is the God of the hunt and provided food to the ancestors.

- The Pentagram is a 5-pointed star. It is their symbol which represents the four elements: Earth, Air, Fire and Water. Also represents the eternal circle, the never-ending renewal of life.

Patti Wigington, a paganism expert who writes for Learn Religions, clarifies what is Wiccan, witch, and pagan:

> Wicca is a tradition of witchcraft that was brought to the public by Gerald Gardner in the 1950s. There is a great deal of debate among the Pagan community about whether or not Wicca is truly the same form of Witchcraft that the ancients practiced. Regardless, many people use the terms Wicca and Witchcraft interchangeably. Paganism is an umbrella term used to apply to a number of different earth-based faiths. Wicca falls under that heading, although not all Pagans are Wiccan.
>
> All Wiccans are witches, but not all witches are Wiccans. All Wiccans are Pagans, but not all Pagans are Wiccans. Finally, *some* witches are Pagans, but some are not—and some Pagans practice witchcraft, while others choose not to.

TYPES OF WITCHES

My friend and author of *Growing Up Paranormal* and *The Lee Avenue Haunting*, Donna Parish-Bischoff, relayed to me in personal correspondence her research into the types of witches that modern-day witches may relate to. According to Donna, "If you are not quite sure what box to check off when you ask yourself what type of witch you are, you can always go through each description and see what you gravitate towards. Not every sector is everyone's cup of Joe. You are a unique human and you will know when you know. It's not that difficult honestly. Takes a while until you get the fit right. There is no hurry up and choose one here."

Alexandrian: This tradition was begun in England in the 1960s by Alex Sanders. Sanders used what are known to be slightly changed Gardnerian traditions and calls himself the "King" of Witches. Covens involve both men and women.

British Traditional: Contains a mix of Celtic and Gardnerian beliefs. Covens involve both men and women. One can study a course and receive a degree in British Traditional Witchcraft.

Caledonii: Once known as the Hecatine tradition. Traditional Scottish witchcraft.

Celtic Wicca: Focuses mainly on Celtic and Druidic gods and goddesses (along with a few other Anglo-Saxon pantheons). The rituals are based on Gardnerian traditions with a stronger emphasis on nature. Celtic Wicca also puts much emphasis on working with elementals and nature spirits such as fairies and gnomes. Gods and goddesses are usually called "The Ancient Ones."

Ceremonial witchcraft: This tradition is very exacting in its ritual. All rituals are usually followed by the book, to the letter, and with much ceremony. Little emphasis is put on nature. This tradition may incorporate some Egyptian magic. Quabbalistic magic is often used in ceremonial witchcraft.

Dianic: Dianic can incorporate nearly any magical traditions, but the emphasis is placed on the Goddess only, with little or no mention of God. Known as the "feminist" type of witchcraft.

Druidic: Neo-Druids are polytheistic worshippers of Mother Earth. Extraordinarily little is known today about ancient Druidism, and many gaps in the writings have been found. Modern Druids practice their religion in areas where nature has been preserved—usually wooded areas. Druidic ritual often employs sacrifices to the Mother Goddess. These sacrifices often include grain, sometimes meat. A verse often accompanies these ritual sacrifices, not unlike the following: "Earth Mother, the giver of life, we return to you a measure of the bounty you have provided. May you be enriched, and your wild things are preserved."

Eclectic: An eclectic witch mixes many different traditions to suit their tastes and will not follow any one tradition. Whatever seems to work best for them is what is used, regardless of which magical practice it comes from. One of the most popular types of witches found today.

Gardnerian: Gardnerian witchcraft began in England in the 1950s and is Wiccan. Its founder, Gerald Gardner, was the first to publicize witchcraft to preserve the "old ways."

Hereditary witch: A hereditary witch is a witch who is born into a witch family and brought up learning about witchcraft. Many witches claim to be hereditary witches when, in fact, they are not. You must be brought up in a family of witches to be a hereditary witch.

Kitchen witch: A kitchen witch is one who practices magic having to deal with the home and practical life. Kitchen witches use many spells involving cooking, herbs, and creating magic through crafts. A kitchen witch is very much like a hedge witch (defined below).

Pictish: Pictish witchcraft is nature-based with little emphasis on religion, gods, or goddesses. It is much like Celtic witchcraft, only the traditions are Scottish. Pictish witches perform solitarily and rarely, if ever, work in groups or covens.

Pow-Wow: Here is a term I rarely hear when referring to witchcraft. This tradition is based on old German magic. Today, it is considered a system of faith healing and can be applied to almost any religion.

Seax-Wicca: This tradition was begun in 1973 by Raymond Buckland and works on Saxon principles of religion and magic.

Shaman: It is arguable as to whether shamanism is or is not witchcraft. I include it here because shamanism is a form of paganism. Shamanism does not emphasize religion or pantheon. Shamans work completely with nature: rocks, trees, animals, rivers, etc. Shamans know the Earth and their bodies and minds well and train many long years to become adept at astral travel and healing.

Solitary witch: Solitary witches can be practitioners of nearly any magical system. A solitary works alone and does not join a group or coven. Often, solitaries choose to mix different systems, much like an eclectic witch. Solitaries can also form their own religious beliefs, as the rules of a coven do not bind them.

Strega: This type of witchcraft is said to have been started by a woman named Aradia in Italy in 1353. Aradia is known in some traditions as the "Goddess of Witches."

Teutonic: A Nordic tradition of witchcraft that includes beliefs and practices from many cultures, including Swedish, Dutch, and Icelandic.

Wicca: Probably the most popular form of witchcraft. Wicca is highly religious and has a good balance between religion/ceremonial magic and nature. Wiccans believe in a God and Goddess who are equal in all things, although some may lean more towards the Dianic form of Wicca, worshipping only the Goddess or lowering God to an "assistant" status. Wiccans commonly form covens and rarely work alone.

"Your head will spin, trying to figure out where you fit in," Donna says. "Which journey suits you? It's not one size fits all. There is this great spiritual journey, and all it has to offer, and then there is YOU! And all you have to offer it. Make no mistake, once you embark, you may say oh wait, this is not what I thought it was—where do I get off? Is there another choice? The answer is sure you have a choice, never let anyone tell you differently."

The other types of witches that one may come across are:

Elemental witches: Work with four major elements—earth, water, air, and fire—and the different correspondences associated with them, which include plants, elements, and colors.

Green witches: Skilled in working with herbs and botanicals and adept at all things pertaining to gardening in their workings. They tend to also be mostly solitary and focus on healing.

Hedge witches: Tend to be solitary and work with nature, communicating with the other side, which is sometimes referred to as "the other side of the hedge."

Star witches: Focus on the stars, constellations, and astrology, and are frequently adept at astral projection.

Water witches: Connected to just that—bodies of water—and may use scrying in their workings.

In addition to types of practitioners of witchcraft, significant special talents are held by them also:

Aerokinesis is manipulating air and wind.

Chlorokinesis is manipulating botanicals.

Chronokinesis is manipulating time.

Electrokineses is manipulating and transmitting electricity and lightning.

Geokinesis is manipulating all of Earth's materials such as lava, sand, and stone.

Hydrokinesis is manipulating water in all of its forms: solid, liquid, and gas.

Photokineses is manipulating light.

Pyrokinesis is manipulating fire and heat.

WITCHES IN THE TWENTY-FIRST CENTURY

Since the early 2000s, paratourism—tourism generated by paranormal places—has been steeply on the rise. In 2014, Krystal Madison created the Sleepy Hollow Festival of Witches, inspired by Hulda the Witch, bringing practitioners from all over the country together to celebrate Halloween, culminating in a Witches Ball. With 2020 and 2021 impacted by COVID-19, the festival also began offering year-round online live classes in the Craft.

In 2015, Marylou Knull created the Witches Crawl in Hudson, where local ladies in witch wear tour local restaurants and pubs on famed historic Warren Street during Halloween week. The event raises money for local charities including Columbia Memorial Hospital and the Columbia-Greene Domestic Violence Program.

Today because of the internet and Facebook, it's easier than ever to be connected. The Facebook page for the group Witches of New York offers a virtual way to connect for many practitioners of witchcraft who may wish to interact with fellow witches but also remain solitary or not gather in person, partially due to COVID. This group focuses on aspects related to growth, such as encouraging journaling and shadow work, Tea and Tarot Tuesdays, and beginning in September of 2021, a monthly book club. The club's first book to read was Scott Cunningham's well-known *Wicca*, meant to connect witches of all experience levels and also give guidance to those just starting to navigate the Craft.

In 2018, beauty brand Sephora faced an outpouring of controversy for its planned nine-piece "Witch Starter Kit," which was to include a tarot deck, sage, and crystals and sell for $42. The kit, which was created by a company called Pinrose, was set to launch in October no less, and was offensive to modern witches who felt that Sephora was disrespecting their craft and was trying to capitalize on their belief system with a product the company might have considered "trendy."

Modern witches felt that the kit mocked their religion, and that the items to be included in it were stereotypical of how witches are misunderstood, and these stereotypes are what witches have been trying to move away from. They felt used by a large company and that Sephora was trying to mass-market synthetic products and abuse what witches considered sacred.

Witches in upstate New York. Photograph by Elizabeth Goodermote, e.goodermote_artist

New York witches that I spoke to had a variety of responses to the kit and remembered how they felt at the time. Andrew Weinstein commented, "Terrible idea, a makeup company with no background in witchcraft had no business doing that. Plus, they were selling white sage, which historically has been appropriated from Native American practices, and also stolen from Native lands to be sold by non-native businesses. Witchcraft is not a trend or a fad. For a lot of people, it is their ancestral practices, and to cheapen it the way Sephora did was inexcusable."

On Twitter and other social media platforms, however, many were quick to voice the opposite opinion—that Wicca is a religion but witchcraft is a practice, and so they saw nothing wrong with bringing a kit to potential new practitioners, making items more available to a broader network of people.

Courtney MacDonald shared her opinion with me: "Larger companies do have a responsibility to their consumers to provide products they believe in and want to share with the world. My personal opinion on the kit was that it was cute. A younger, makeup obsessed version of myself would have been delighted to find something like this in a well known store. But at this point in my life I don't feel strongly one way or another. There was nothing included in that kit that would cause someone to be able to cause any ill will without knowledge of the tools. And anyone who has that kind of knowledge wasn't interested in a starter kit. I say, let people enjoy things. Let that be a young person's first step into spirituality. I certainly would have welcomed it when I was 13/14 years old."

Taneal Stewart put this positive outlook forward: "Given the nature of the item 'starter kit' for a lot of buyers, that's going to be their first foray into Wicca. I'm not against it, because it provides access to witchcraft to those who might not have come into contact with it so directly before. Same with all the big brand stores selling witchcraft items. I believe it's just a starting point, it plants a seed inside someone, and if they're meant to follow that path, they'll find their way to more information, and in turn support smaller practitioners for supplies—it does nothing but drive demand, which eventually does turn into profit for wiccan businesses."

From central New York, Tracy Ann Edson and Storm Anderson shared their opinions: "Think it's a great idea . . . We all have done spell casting whether we know it or not . . . and if this 'normalizes' what my family practices and believes I am all for it . . . I don't believe you have to go into a specialty shop to be a practitioner . . . Barnes and Nobles sells terrific tarot decks, books, rune sets . . . People need to get back to the essence that they are the magick." And, "There's something to be said for seeking out the magical, the esoteric, and the occult rather than being spoon fed watered down versions. Witches don't need to be recruited. If it's something one feels in their blood, like the innate urge to create by naturally born Artists, then they'll find their way. Witches also don't require some special understanding or broad acceptance. I much prefer a bit of the mystery, and that some even fear it. Take that away and you take away power. Most importantly, Witches don't need, nor should they want, a bunch of Muggles all wanting to get on board some trendy instawitch train. Operate the shops, write the books, and offer some classes. If they were meant to be, if they were born to be Witches, they'll find their way."

Pinrose was forced to rethink their marketing fail and issued this apology after deciding against producing the starter kit: "First and foremost, to those who have shared their disappointment or taken offense to this product, we apologize profoundly. This was not our intent. We thank you for communicating with us and expressing your feelings. We hear you; we will not be manufacturing or making this product available for sale. Our intention for the product was to create something that celebrates wellness, personal ceremony, and intention setting with a focus on using fragrance as a beauty ritual."

Time magazine, the *New York Times*, the *Guardian*, *New York* magazine, *Teen Vogue*, and the *New York Post* have recently featured articles on witches in what's being referred to as the "Witch Wave"—a resurgence in the fascination with witches.

The *New York Post*'s article was about Liz Pressman, a news librarian at the *Post* who had been fired after a coworker complained about the goddess pendant Liz had worn to the office. Now Liz says, "Kids seem to know witches are safe and cool. They feel our energies. Meanwhile, this new public embrace of witchcraft makes me feel warm and appreciated. This week, I was buying a lot of dried fruit and bread from my local deli in the run-up to Samhain. When I told the owner that I needed them for offerings, he told me, 'Happy Holidays!' "

VERONICA VARLOW AND HER MAGIC HOUSE

Known not just in New York but worldwide as a burlesque dancer and performance artist, Brooklyn-based Veronica Varlow also has a celebrated upstate witch house known as the Curiosa Magic House, which is written about in this book in more detail in the following chapter. Her website, Love Witch, is devoted to her interests in teaching magic and tarot, and also offers potions and devotions through its online shop. She does Tarot Tuesdays on Instagram and has a new book out in the fall of 2021, *Bohemian Magick*.

After an eight-hour surgery due to a dog attack, Veronica gave up the "cubicle life" to pursue her dreams, which have paid off tremendously. Her website describes her as "a confidence & sensuality coach who has been featured on The Tonight Show, Playboy, CNN and MTV in 150 countries across the globe. She is a love ritualist and a fourth generation intuitive. Her client list includes Chanel, Tiffany & Co., Vogue, Marc Jacobs, Creative Time with David Byrne, and the Whitney Museum."

Veronica was hugely impacted by her grandmother's practices, which were pointed out to her by a friend after her grandmother's passing as those of a witch. It was this friend who gave Veronica her first book on witchcraft. The term *witch* startled her, making her defensive at first, as is often our modern-day reaction to that label. Over time, however, Veronica made peace with and embraced the witch. As she has said, "Other kids got into drugs, I got deeper and deeper into magic."

On October 31, 2020, Veronica married David Garfinkel, with whom she runs a coven at the Chelsea Hotel in New York City.

JOE NETHERWORLD AND THE HALLOWEEN HOUSE

Interesting people have more to offer.

—*Joe Netherworld*

Joe Netherworld (Joe Mendillo) made his mark on upstate New York, becoming known as "America's Favorite Satanist." His story would then become known the world over as well.

Joe's story, and that of his house, would be covered by the *New York Times*, *New York Post*, *Daily Mail*, and *Guardian*, among other notable publications. His house was a renovated, restored, former crack house in Poughkeepsie. Previously, it had also been a boardinghouse/halfway house for people getting out of prison and returning to society. It became the famous Halloween House to outsiders, but to those who knew Joe well, it was the House of Netherworld, which he described as "New Orleans, swampy, witchy, cool."

Certain times of the year were a drag for Joe: "In January it's tedious being home bound instead of being outside with my plants. It's a low time of year." But his house was a sanctuary to many who needed refuge and was a home full of love, and hosted a steady stream of people who stayed there, dined there, and helped Joe with various renovation projects.

Longtime friend Falon, who met Joe through mutual friends in the 1990s while Joe lived in Peekskill, explained that walking into Joe's house was like walking into his mind and also said that "Joe could walk on many grounds and with aplomb." Joe's sister Angella shared with me, "He took people in like an old-school Italian."

Joe and his house raised eyebrows at first, like many different newcomers in any region, but he was a very kind and helpful neighbor and became much loved. He made an unsafe neighborhood safe and festive again, especially during Halloween, with his English bulldog, Medusa. Joe even kept peacocks. Many Poughkeepsie neighborhoods had no Halloween decorations or trick-or-treaters, so they came to Joe's house. His Halloween candy handout philosophy was clear: "My rules are now known through-out the land. Devils, Witches and skeletons get double candy. Princesses, cheerleaders and good guys get second rate candy and if you have no costume and turn your back on me and expect me to put candy in your bag I will steal from you."

In October 2014 in one his videos, Joe mentioned his unhappiness with the "war on Halloween people": "The magic of Halloween is being lost on these people. People interacting, dressing up, masquerading, celebrating, going door to door—it's not an anti-Christian holiday. Don't get in the way of people being people."

With his birthday being April 29, he was born just a day before Walpurgisnacht (Night of the Witches)—the time when witches gather for the Great Sabbath of the year. Walpurgisnacht, which falls so close to Beltane (May 1), is thought to be the oldest known holiday and is one of the two most important fire festivals, celebrated by gathering just before midnight at a crossroads with a large bonfire. It is also a fertility festival, with dancing and lovemaking until the Horned God emerges. Ointments made with magical qualities are applied to all parts of one's body. Walpurgisnacht, like Samhain/Halloween, was also considered a time when the veil between this and the Netherworld was at its thinnest.

Joe Netherworld welcomed all into his home. He was someone people describe as being open, a person you could have tea with and he'd listen to your problems.

From a young age, Joe was part of the "witches and weirdos" set of peers, as he described them. He later became a set designer and also learned jewelry making and sold his wares at the Chiller Festival. He was also an art director for Rock Shots Greeting Cards.

"A million years ago I wandered into a West Village antique store & saw this Mechagodzilla ring for sale. The shopkeeper told me, 'It was made by a local artist named Joe Netherworld. Have you heard of him?' wrote Joe Babbo on Joe Netherworld's Facebook page, where he shared a photo of the ring.

One of Joe's proudest moments came from receiving a picture from Vincent Price of him at his home wearing the ring Joe had made for him.

I interviewed many people for this book who shared their feelings and memories about Joe. Although I didn't get to meet him before he passed, I found that I had several friends in common with him, making not having had the chance to meet and interview him for this book even more bittersweet.

Julia Drahos, owner of Miss Fanny's Victorian Party House, became friends with Joe through doing various events with him over the years and sharing mutual friends. She described him as being a cross between Vincent Price and Martha Stewart; his many talents included being a great gardener. "He threw terrific parties," Julie said. "Satanism was just about being an atheist. The Witchcraft District initiated by him was a result of finding that many of his surrounding neighbors shared his same belief system."

A former neighbor recalled that Joe "never saw himself as being persecuted and certainly not as a victim. As a Satanist, and self-proclaimed male witch, he lived his life to the fullest and did his best to help many people to find acceptance."

The people at Adams Fairacre Farm fondly remember Joe's visits, when he would buy produce for parties but also belladonna, toad lilies, monkshood, devil's weed, and all the ingredients to make "Witches Flying Oil."

Joe described himself as a mostly good witch, although sometimes a little bad, as he wasn't above throwing a curse. With a turkey quill found in a cemetery, he wrote his own blessings and curses in his personal Book of Shadows. "True witchcraft is a natural art; where we seek to change reality, bend time, and change outcomes," he was fond of saying.

Joe created a video series focusing on the paranormal and witchcraft, filmed in his dining room, called *The Dark Side*, where he spoke of ancient traditions and folklore. Flying ointment he described as being made of deadly nightshade botanicals and hallucinogenic herbs mixed with fats, applied to a broom and subsequently ingested by a witch through her broom ride.

Joe was fond of upstate New York's Hulda, describing her as "an old-world witch." He commissioned a wooden witch, carved from an old elm tree struck by lightning that had fallen on a cemetery fence, to watch over and protect his home. She was called Hulda.

Perhaps Joe was descended from a long line of Italian witches; his ancestors came from Benevento, Italy, known as the "place of witches." One of his favorite drinks was a liquor called Strega, witch liquor, made from seventy-one botanicals of the Benevento region of Campania.

Unguent, unguent,
me to the walnut tree of Benevento,
Under the water and under the wind,
under all bad weather.

The Benevento witches were known to use this flying spell, documented during witch trials there. Allegedly, they anointed themselves with an unguent and took off flying on stormy nights, their preferred time. As they were believed to enter a home under its door, villagers took to placing a broom and salt on the threshold, the belief being that a witch couldn't enter without counting all the broom's fibers and all the grains of salt. These beliefs surrounding brooms and salt were then brought to America by ancestors long ago.

In his eighteen-room Gothic-style house, Joe collected Ouija boards and had one in every room. He knew that witch boards had been around for centuries, maybe longer, and are believed to open portals.

One particular witch board Joe told of acquiring while at a yard sale, where he met an old lady who asked him to take it off her hands. She told him the board's story. She and her sister played with it frequently until her sister died of tuberculosis. Keeping the board as a memento, she would play with it, trying to communicate with her departed sister, until it kept spelling out terrible things. She stopped using the board and left it propped in a window with a candle nearby. One day the Ouija board apparently flipped and knocked the lit candle over, starting a house fire where the only thing not to completely burn in the room was the Ouija board itself. Joe took the board from this lady and kept it because of its story.

Another scary item long associated with witchcraft is the voodoo doll, or poppet. Joe had a vast collection of these dolls from all over, along with some he had made himself. Transferring one's energy to the voodoo doll, one would gather items connected to a person and then the doll becomes a symbol of that person. A note containing the intentions for the person would be pinned to the doll, which would then ideally be placed in the person's home.

One of Joe's earliest experiences with such a doll came in high school. A quarterback bully who was mean to Joe's best friend became the object of a voodoo doll made by them, with one of its legs pinned up behind its back. The next day at school, they learned that the jock had broken his leg, sidelining his football career. "A curse," Joe explained, "is sometimes thrown to re-create balance in the Universe and right wrongs, and they have worked. We don't always know how they work, but they do work."

Like many witches, Joe had a familiar. It was a pet toad who later was petrified upon its passing, preserved and placed on an altar in his home.

But with the sweet comes the sour, as they say. Persecution for different beliefs still arises in modern times. Just walk down any street wearing a pentacle or pentagram as a necklace, and see what happens.

Harkening back to the Burning Times, sadly in January 2021 Joe's house would burn; perhaps motivated by religious persecution, a hate crime was committed. Or maybe someone who had wanted the house after Joe's passing is responsible. Until the arsonist is found, we can't know the true motive of this fire.

A friend who had made a film on Joe and his house for Vassar College related to me, "I'm so glad you enjoyed the film about Joe. He was such a special person, and an excellent witch. I really miss him and can't believe he AND his house are gone. What a tragedy. Did they ever find out who did it? I remember when I was filming with him, 12 years ago now, and he was saying that he'd been harassed a couple of times by a nearby christian church group. I can't remember the details, but recall they maybe did some vandalizing on his porch. I wondered if it was the same people. In many ways, Joe was that house. It was an external representation of his spirit. I felt honored to be welcomed inside and into his world."

The house, built in the mid-1800s, was subsequently owned by Joe's companion Matthew Camp after his passing. Tim Martinez was among the first to let others know the details after the fire. "Matthew had *just* finished moving all of his belongings into the House along with his roommate Six Carter," he said. "They lost everything. They barely made it out alive while the House burned for 3 hours."

Matthew escaped the home in the early morning hours after it was set ablaze by arson, and the house was "burned down to its bones" according to the *Poughkeepsie Journal*. On this bitter January morning, Matthew escaped with just the clothes he was wearing along with his phone, making it out just in time.

A GoFundMe was set up after the tragedy, raising $60,000. Matthew shared on social media what must have been a terrifying experience and what no one should ever have to experience: "January 14, 2021. An arsonist poured gasoline on the front porch of my home and set it on fire in an apparent hate crime. I was asleep inside. I am alive to face this person one day but everything I have ever owned is gone. Share this story because queer people are still under attack all over the world. Our voices will not be silenced. Right now I'm just living day to day trying to piece together what's left. If you are able to help there's a link in my bio. Thank you for the love and support and continued fight to keep our queer families safe."

Matthew is a well-known LGBTQ performer. That kind of fame can also bring negative attention, and possibly attract jealous people and stalkers. Another possible motivation for the fire could be anti-LGBTQ sentiment.

Video footage shows a person dousing the house with cans of gasoline and then setting it ablaze around 5:00 a.m. Almost exactly a year after the tragedy of Joe's passing in January 2020, his house too would pass.

"It was a home that promoted the Church of Satan," said city councilman Chris Petsas. "A lot of devil sculptures and paraphernalia. It was extraordinarily different. It wasn't your normal home."

After this tragedy many local people were interviewed by the *Poughkeepsie Journal*. "Some 'people of faith' are intolerant, and typically ignorant, of other belief systems," a neighbor said to the newspaper. "But Joe did not focus on bigoted people. Instead, he chose to be a vibrant part of Poughkeepsie. In 2013, Joe conducted the first legally recognized same-sex wedding in New York State by a Satanic clergyman. It currently seems unlikely that the home could be restored, due to the severe fire damage, but one day a 'pocket park' could possibly arise on that space."

People who do the research and look into what Joe's religion consisted of would learn that it is not devil worship, but an atheist philosophy of individualism and fulfillment.

The *New York Times* ran a story about the tragedy, where Isis Vermouth said the arson felt like a "terror attack. Everybody's in shock and everyone in the neighborhood is worried. Whoever did this is going to be hexed by all of us. I feel like this was definitely malicious. Someone showed up in a hazmat suit and poured two huge jugs of gasoline on the porch while everyone was sleeping."

According to the *Daily Mail* (UK), "The Church of Satan was founded in 1966 by the late Anton Szandor LaVey in San Francisco, as a 'skeptical atheist' philosophy focused on individualism and enlightenment. It did not worship the devil. After Szandor LaVey's death in 1997 a new leader was appointed and the headquarters moved to Hells Kitchen in New York, before he was 'inspired' by Mendillo to move it to Poughkeepsie."

On the morning of the fire, the City of Poughkeepsie Historic District and Landmark Preservation Commission wasted no time in lamenting the loss of the home along with the home's history:

Early this morning the City of Poughkeepsie Fire Department valiantly saved the residents of 27 South Clinton Street but the historic Victorian home succumbed to suspected arson. We are truly grateful no lives were lost in this horrific blaze and thank all of the local fire departments who worked to extinguish and contain this devastating fire.

As of late this stately residence at the intersection of South Clinton Street and Church Street was often referred to as the "Halloween House." However, let history remember that for over 150 years this building commanded a significant presence on this corner. Since urban renewal recreated this section of Church Street into the east/west arterial, it has seized the attention of drivers.

William Quintard boarded at the Northern Hotel before he achieved success as a jeweler in Poughkeepsie. In 1870 he built his Carpenter Gothic house at 27 South Clinton Street, a new architectural jewel in this neighborhood. In 1891 he added a two story addition.

Quintard's home was impressive with its decorative, architectural details including brackets, a crowning center peak over a prominent bay window and a wide, inviting porch with columns. These vibrant characteristics always served as a visual reminder of the 19th century development of Victorian homes occurring on Poughkeepsie's east side. Poised as a striking entry to South Clinton Street it was an integral part of a beautiful neighborhood that continues to represent excellent examples of our architectural heritage.

Even in its deeper shade of teal and copious growth of greenery and vines, this whimsical home maintained the contour of its original Victorian elegance. It reminded us of an age when the addition of architectural features such as patterned brick work, transom windows and scrollsaw balustrades were hallmarks of beauty on our city's streets.

Joe's home had come to be known as the Halloween House. According to friends and family, he was a big Halloween fan. He would put up his countdown clock on the front porch several months before Halloween, counting down the days. He had a pumpkin figure similar to a jack-o'-lantern man that was made of twisted branches with a pumpkin head on it. Joe felt that keeping his house spooky might help to protect it because the neighborhood was scary when he bought it. Apparently the post office and FedEx wouldn't deliver mail to his home address.

Joe's friends and family say that the term *Witchcraft District* was something that Joe coined to mean the state of mind of neighbors living there. Joe's house contained his amazing collections—everything from oddities to artwork and sculpture—which were cataloged by his friend Falon and kept in storage when Joe became ill. One of the most remembered things about Joe was how he took darkness and made it be known that it wasn't what people thought it to be. He was light, as some recall. A Renaissance man.

Interesting too was an image of a hand print on a doorway that Joe had kept. The prior owner had passed away in the house due to a large fire that took place there.

I was fortunate to be able to speak with a member of Joe Netherworld's family, his sister Angella, who shared personal details despite the profound sadness of her loss—memories of their childhoods, his home, his philosophy. "There were misconceptions of Joe," she said. "He actually never did drugs of any kind and he was very sweet. But now looking back, it's hard to believe that Joey used to always say referring to his house, 'After I'm gone just take a match and burn it down.'"

Angella was at Joe's house the day after his passing and was disheartened by the many curiosity seekers "picking over its bones" and asking if they could have some of his possessions or the house itself. One couple from California wished to buy it and turn it into a museum. "Joey wouldn't have wanted that," his sister said.

"Joey had Shawn Poirer's hat on a mantle; people were trying to take stuff, get a piece of him," Angella told me.

The three hundred koi fish in Joe's pond were killed by the fire-retardant chemicals; the peacocks were rescued and now live on a farm in upstate New York. Sadly, Joe's library was also completely destroyed; it had housed many first-edition and hard-to-find occult books.

It will be left to Matthew Camp to decide what is next for the property. "The property is still in Camp's name. He and the community intend to turn it into a park and eventually erect a statue of cult filmmaker and former Poughkeepsie resident Ed Wood, an important figure for Mendillo," reports Jessica Chapp for the *Times Union*, Albany.

Dena Sewell, a friend of Joe's, said of him: "In my mind's eye, I imagine he is having a jolly good time sipping fancy cocktails with legions of beautiful fallen angels and demons as he did when he was in our realm. When he exited this world he took a huge piece of my heart."

There are many *The Dark Side* YouTube videos remaining to remember Joe Netherworld by, and his personal Facebook page is forever. We also have Vicki Marquette's 2009 Vassar College film/ interview on Joe, *America's Favorite Satanist*, and we are thankful that all of these survive.

From one of Joe's Daily Tarot readings: "The power of the universe is in your flesh. Be one with your power and relish the fleshy world. Make physical changes and praise magic and supernatural power in your life. Actively refute societal control over your will and accept yourself as god of your own universe. Rise up and rule."

The Witchcraft District Bazaar is a shop at 8 Carmel Place, Poughkeepsie, created by witch, creative, and seamstress Priestess

Renee M. Anderson and Renee's husband, warlock and artist Reverend A. W. Storm Anderson. The Bazaar offers a selections of products to meet the needs of different witch paths, with hand-crafted works, original art, occult items, ritual tools and altar pieces, jewelry, books, tarot, dried organic herbs, incense, healing crystals, decor, and commemorative novelties to remember the unique area, including branded items, apparel, and accessories to display pride in Weird Poughkeepsie.

Known as the King and Queen of Halloween, both Storm and Renee told me of their fondness of Joe Netherworld and their inspiration to create the Bazaar in personal correspondences with me and also on the shop's website: "The moniker 'Witchcraft District' endured, evolved, has continued to garner attention, and has expanded beyond the original neighborhood. It's a state of mind, a concept that extends to any house with inhabitants that find they resonate with a witchy lifestyle, spooky things, and reflect that in their aesthetic and creative self-expression. Now, Witchcraft District has become a nickname synonymous with Poughkeepsie! It only seemed fitting that the Witchcraft District have its own distinctive placard. Experienced designer and Witchcraft District resident Falon Eduard Blutig used her skill and talent to create a wonderful and perfectly fitting plaque that may now be seen on many homes in the area."

On the day Joe died, his sister Angella went back to her New York City apartment and tried to process it all. In the garden, at the back of her home, she heard a noise. There, in the garden, was a huge crow eating a rat. Angella remarked to me that not only was it rare to see a large crow like that in a back garden, but it almost seemed to her like it was Joe, grossing her out like siblings growing up do to one another, and it was his way of saying "Now I'm outta here" as the crow took off.

The grave calls everything back to it, as Joe himself would have said.

MARGOT ADLER AND DRAWING DOWN THE MOON

Another truly inspiring person where witchcraft is concerned is Margot Adler, a leading figure in American paganism. I did not have the opportunity to meet her, but on the journey of writing this book discovered that she and I had mutual friends, which makes it even more poignant. Though our paths did not cross, I am happy to have in my collection her book *Drawing Down the Moon: Witches, Druids, Goddess-Worshippers, and Other Pagans in America Today.*

"Drawing down the moon" is a term and ritual many contemporary Wiccans are familiar with, where during the ritual a coven's High Priestess enters into a trance asking that the Goddess or Triple Goddess, symbolized by the Moon, enter her body, speaking through her.

Margot Adler, New York City resident, practicing pagan, and NPR correspondent, passed away in 2014. Her book *Drawing Down the Moon*, written in 1979 and published on All Hallows' Eve, was considered groundbreaking at the time and is still highly recommended by the pagan community today.

The *New York Times* Book Review made the best point when it stated, "Given the lurid connotations neopaganism has acquired ... *Drawing Down the Moon* is a healthy corrective."

The author herself said that the message of the book is "that the spiritual world is like the natural world—only diversity will save it."

In the 1970s, Margot became High Priestess of a Gardnerian coven, Iargalon. She believed in the power of ritual to connect those in a community to the spiritual connection of the natural world.

Her book is about the pagan resurgence and is "the only detailed history of Neo-Paganism in the United States," as Margot stated in 1986. The author said that the pagan resurgence did not include Satanists. I read the book hearing her voice, as I had had the opportunity to listen to radio interviews of Margot while she was still with us. *Drawing Down the Moon* is still in print and remains a heavily researched passion and lasting legacy of the author. The book took a while to research and write during the time of internet-free communication and was a result of her travels interviewing covens and gatherings in the United States, Canada, and Great Britain. It was written largely in the Frederick Lewis Allen Room of the New York Public Library, which she enjoyed as being very welcoming.

One of Margot's first steps in crafting her book was to have a lengthy questionnaire published in the neo-pagan journal *Green Egg*, receiving hundreds of pages of responses. In 1985 a new, updated questionnaire was published in *Panegyria*, garnering 195 responses. It was Margot's experience as well that in modern times many people still associated the words *witchcraft*, *magic*, and *occult* with negative connotations. She explained that witches, according to the modern religion definition, are members of a polytheistic nature-based religion, living peaceful, somewhat ordinary lives, with rituals marking seasonal turns of the wheel of the year.

In understanding the definition and purpose of magic, she stated it in this way: "Magic is a convenient word for a whole collection of techniques, all of which involve the mind. We might conceive of these techniques as including the mobilization of confidence, will and emotion brought about by the recognition of necessity; the use of imaginative faculties, particularly the ability to visualize; in order to begin to understand how other beings function in nature so that we can use this knowledge to achieve necessarily ends." And witches, and witchcraft, Margot said, "unlock a set of explosive associations that inspire unease if not fear."

Margot recalled in her book the time an Essex coven sent her a tape recording of rituals, one being "the drawing down of the moon" with the Triple Goddess invoked. A priestess then in a trance speaks, becoming the Goddess. Margot believed that people do not convert to paganism, but rather "accept, reaffirm, and extend a very old experience; allowing certain kinds of feelings and ways of being back into their lives."

Many modern practitioners prefer the word *Craft* over witchcraft, as witchcraft to some implies a dead version of an old faith, while Craft is more about the *way* of practicing. Some practitioners wish to identify with ancient pre-Christian predecessors but many do not, wishing to be thought of and practicing in more modern terms.

Margot's reasons for joining the pagan community were "out of a search for a celebratory, ecological nature religion that would appease my hunger for the beauty of ancient myths and visions without strangling my mind with dogmas or cutting off the continuing flow of many doubts." In the 1970s she captured how many in the pagan community felt about the word *witch* and whether or not it would ever be reclaimed. The overall consensus was that the word "carries a part of our past. It would be dangerous to forget it and leave it behind." But she also felt that "the most important argument against the word witch is that it just doesn't communicate the reality of the Pagan experience to most of the public, whereas a less loaded word often does. There is also the dilemma that not even everybody in the Craft means the same thing by the term witch." She found that many would only use the term with people they trusted, preferring at first to describe themselves as pagan or Wiccan.

In a 2010 interview on *Blog Talk Radio* with Karen Tate, Margot gave her opinions on what had changed in the past twenty years for pagans and what she felt was coming. In a very spirited conversation she was asked about writing this still important and influential book. When asked if it was a hard book to write, she explained how in the 1970s there was sporadic communication, unlike the ease of today's internet. There were printed newsletters, and she was a newbie pagan seeking larger groups of like-minded people. Quite by chance, she met a literary agent in a New York City bar and mentioned that she was involved in witchcraft, which caught the interest of the agent. Margot was asked if she ever considered writing a book and replied, "No, the written word terrifies me." The agent was looking for clients and helped Margot put together a proposal that got accepted by a publisher.

Margot was on unemployment at the time, and the book would take three years to complete. She started reaching out and writing to people she knew from newsletters to interview. In 1986 the book was revised, started to get more attention, and took off from there. She also appeared on the *Phil Donahue Show*.

Margot expressed in the radio interview that "there is such a huge amount of contemporary pagans now and by 2002 there were about five thousand websites devoted to paganism. It's a world religion and multigenerational movement. It used to be so secretive and hard to find groups to join. You learned the Craft personally from a teacher. Now, it can be a little impersonal with people being more solitary and learning from the internet. By 1986, there were women's festivals all over the country; we seem to be seeing less of that now." She indicated that she had in her career experienced discrimination by being passed over for opportunities because of her paganism. During her research, she had interviewed a pagan from the Midwest who stated that she believed in not telling her neighbors or coworkers of being pagan, adding that "if they don't know where you live, they can't burn your house down."

As chilling as that was then, it is even more so today when you know what happened to Joe Netherworld's Poughkeepsie house, and that it can very much still occur. Margot stated that most types of persecution were more subtle as to the ways witches were portrayed in films like *The Exorcist* and *Rosemary's Baby*.

"A lot of the Pagan movement today, including a lot of the Wicca movement, is based on going back to our ancestors' traditions or creating them anew—since many of these traditions have been lost," Margot said. "It's an attempt to create a vibrant, juicy contemporary culture based on old sources, on what our ancestors were doing, or at least part of what they were doing, or at least a tiny slice of what they were doing thousands of years ago, but it's also an attempt to bring these traditions into contemporary reality, in ways that are in keeping with democracy and freedom."

Among the scores of people Margot interviewed, there were those who felt that the Craft was about helping people to reclaim spirituality. Many felt that their religion would always remain small, that the "fad of the occult" would pass, and the emphasis was on "practical magic to get various jobs done."

When asked by Karen Tate towards the end of their radio interview "What stokes your passion these days?" Margot replied, "I am in transition these days." Today, a memorial bench in Central Park is installed where she walked frequently and enjoyed bird-watching.

TWO CURRENT UPSTATE PRACTITIONERS AND ENTREPRENEURS

M. A. Phillips is an upstate author and practicing Druid. Her blog ditzydruid.com is where to find her photographs and the inspiration that led to her writing her novels after moving to northern New York, recording her journey as a pagan and Druid in the North Country. Her first, *River Magic* (2020), is an adult magical realism novel set in the beautiful Thousand Islands region of upstate New York, featuring contemporary pagans and a friends-to-lovers romance. "Druidry is my foundation," Phillips says. "It roots and guides me. All my other obligations and hobbies are my branches. My spiritual practice feeds the branches, providing the nourishment and structure for them to flourish. Occasionally, I have to drop a few branches, but that only strengthens the health of the overall tree—me!"

Vanessa Hanks, European shamanic practitioner, folk magic healer, and Reiki master, opened her intuitive practice in a beautiful 1800s cobblestone building on Spirit Highway (Route 5 and 20) in West Bloomfield, New York, called Spirit, Spindle and Root in December 2021. The practice provides various types of intuitive readings, healings (folk magic, shamanic, spirit, elemental, and energy/Reiki healings), services for ghost-related issues, and classes on American folk magic, spirit work, European shamanic, folk and pagan practices, healing, and more. The shop sells a variety of items to support magical, intuitive, and shamanic practice; healing work; and divination, along with artwork, jewelry, gifts, and occult antiques.

In personal correspondence with me, Vanessa shared her love of folk witchcraft, which for her "is the remnants of a past shamanic tradition of my ancestors. America magic traditions are like our country, a melding of the different cultures that came together in a certain place. In New York, it has been hidden because it was eclipsed in the 1800s by Spiritualism (and other factors). But remnants of it can still be found and I am working to collect what I am calling 'Granny Apple Magic of New York' because it shares some common traits with other American-born magical traditions. But in general, folk magic is focused on spirits, lore & land. But my relationship with spirits is at its core and I am guided by them more than any magical system."

On her Instagram feed, Vanessa wrote about upstate New York witch Jane Buell from the early 1900s and also wrote on her philosophy:

Jane told a folklorist that sprigs of witch hazel would assume the form of a bow and arrow, and shoot the witch tormenting her with pneumonia. She described witch hazel as devious in character and used it for divining rods to find underground springs, lost items and stolen property.

I am a folklorist at heart. I have been studying the hidden folk magic tradition and history here in New York and plan to share some of what I learn through posts like this on "witch-hazel." I love the idea that witch-hazel has a personality. As a shamanic and folk magic practitioner, my worldview is "animistic," meaning that all things have a spirit, medicine and wisdom to share. I also love the idea that the sprigs of witch-hazel will form a bow and arrow and "shoot" a hexing witch. This reminds me of the idea of elf-shot and perhaps "white witch" Jane was looking to do a bit of reverse work by shooting the hex back at the sending witch! Reversal work is an important magical skill. I want to share shamanism, paganism and folk witchcraft paths because they have deeply resonated with me as my worldview is "animistic," meaning that I believe that all things in nature and life have a spirit, wisdom and medicine. If we go back far enough in any part of the world, people honored and were in relationship with nature and its spirits as the backbone of their spirituality. I believe the diverse shamanic, pagan and witchcraft traditions globally can help to bring us back to a time when humans lived in greater balance with the natural and spirited worlds. I believe an animistic perspective in particular can help to heal some of the harm that humans have done to nature and the planet by remembering that we are not above anything in nature—but instead are a part of it, in an ecosystem that must be balanced to be healthy. Through my store, services and classes, I want to help people to reconnect with a forgotten past of living in flow with nature and spirits, but in a way that is accessible to people living today. I am interested in helping others learn how to work with energy and spirits for self-discovery, spiritual growth, personal healing, and to co-create a life of greater holistic wellness, fulfillment and balance. I have a deep appreciation for American folk magic and healing. It often stems from people who were oppressed, disenfranchised and on the fringes of society due to race, poverty, gender or geographic isolation. It was a way to try and change sometimes impossible circumstances such as slavery, oppression, lack of means, sickness, weather, and more. Other times, it was to influence daily life such as one's love, luck, health, or to successfully grow crops or rear livestock. I love folk magic because it is the magic of the diverse peoples that made and make up our country. And in my opinion, those who historically practiced it in its many forms, developed powerful magic to help maneuver and take some control of an unpredictable world that was not always going to give them a fair shake. The real needs, emotions and even desperation of our predecessors is what has given folk magic its power. I believe to honor them—including their struggles and trials—I must honor the equality of all people. And because I believe in animism, honor the equality of all things. I carry this belief system with me as a practicing folk witch.

WITCHES IN GALLERIES

September Gallery poster for April 22, 2017, Witches event. Courtesy of Kristen Dodge

In 2017, the September Gallery in Hudson, New York, held an exhibition of witchcraft-based art. In the lead-up to the show, associate professor of art history at Bard College Susan Aberth described the upcoming show. Her specialties are Latin American art, Surrealism, and occultism.

About *Witches* Aberth said: "*Witches*, an exhibition at September, presents five artists whose working processes and artwork either directly employs or indirectly suggests magical intentions. The term 'witch' has always stood for feminine subversive forces, acting either outside of or in opposition to the oppressive rules of patriarchy. Furthermore, an integral part of witchcraft entails the creation of specially charged objects meant to facilitate magical objectives, such as the rectification of injustices, protection from harm, or the expansion of consciousness. Marjorie Cameron (1922–1995), the great American artist, poet and occultist, serves as the presiding muse of the show with four extraordinary works on paper."

The night of the opening the scene was set with a ritual to create a specific mood, whereas afterwards author Pam Grossman gave a talk on the image of the witch in art. Professor K. A. Laity, who teaches medieval literature and splits her time between Hudson, New York, and Dundee, Scotland, took many of the gallery opening's photographs.

In 2012, Brooklyn's Observatory held the exhibition *Sigils and Signs*, curated by Pam Grossman. This group show of fourteen artists demonstrated the beauty of symbols and mandalas seen throughout history in many major religions.

WICCAN AND WITCH ORGANIZATIONS

Reverend Starr RavenHawk of the Wiccan Family Temple, New York City.
Courtesy of the Wiccan Family Temple

The website Untapped New York asks us, "Ever fantasized about attending New York City's very own Hogwarts?"

New York City's Wiccan Family Temple Academy of Pagan Studies exists to educate current and new practitioners of the Craft since 2008. The fundamentals of Wicca are taught as well as Introduction to Magick, Introduction to Rituals, and Sacred Space, Altars, and Tools. The center offers a free library and a haunted house at Halloween as well. Students are accepted year-round for classes with affordable rates.

The academy's informative website answers many basic questions about witches and witchcraft, and explains, "Our principle tenets teach us to have an active role in our lives. We are pacifists but hardly inactive when it comes to protecting ourselves. We use our Magick and our science to get out of harm's way and to help others do the same. We do not return harm or incorrect energy to those that wish it upon us, we neutralize it so it can harm none or transmutes it to fortify our energies. It is best to make the fire 'cease to be' than to drown it with water. A Witch must learn to take care of themselves before they can help others in any meaningful way. This is not selfish, but practical. You would want your surgeon to be at their best before embarking on a complex operation, Witches view life in this way."

One question that arises frequently is the use of magick versus magic, which is explained on their website: "We do not use the word magic, as it is the skill used for amusement. Magick is the global term for the force at work behind The Craft and the traditions of many who are not Witches, such as in the American Indian tradition and others."

The Cabot Kent Hermetic Temple updated text of *The Witches Federal Law Memorandum* in the summer of 2020, with thanks to Patricia A. Barki, legal intern, Legal Department of the Cabot Kent Hermetic Temple, for her research and authorship of the law memorandum. The memorandum illustrates how witchcraft is a protected religion in the United States by the Constitution. The Church of Wicca (or Witchcraft) is a religion under the First Amendment. This memorandum is an important document available to all and easily found thanks to the internet.

The Council of American Witches was formed by Carl Llewellyn Weschcke, president of Llewellyn Publishing, in 1974. Comprised of seventy-three witches, its members included Isaac Bonewits, ArchDruid, Rusty Bonewits, and Margot Adler. Although they disbanded later that same year, they created the Thirteen Principles of Belief:

1. We practice rites to attune ourselves with the natural rhythm of life forces marked by the phases of the Moon and the season Quarters and Cross Quarters.
2. We recognize that our intelligence gives us a unique responsibility towards our environment. We seek to live in harmony with Nature, in ecological balance offering fulfillment to life and consciousness within an evolutionary concept.
3. We acknowledge a depth of power far greater than that is apparent to the average person. Because it is far greater than ordinary it is sometimes called "supernatural," but we see it as lying within that which is naturally potential to all.
4. We conceive of the Creative Power in the universe as manifesting through polarity—as masculine and feminine—and that this same Creative Power lies in all people, and functions through the interaction of the masculine and feminine. We value neither above the other, knowing each to be

supportive of the other. We value sex as pleasure, as the symbol and embodiment of life, and as one of the sources of energies used in magickal practice and religious worship.

5. We recognize both outer and inner, or psychological, worlds— sometimes known as the Spiritual World, the Collective Unconscious, Inner Planes, etc.—and we see in the interaction of these two dimensions the basis for paranormal phenomena and magickal exercises. We neglect neither dimension for the other, seeing both as necessary for our fulfillment.

6. We do not recognize any authoritarian hierarchy, but do honor those who teach, respect those who share their greater knowledge and wisdom, and acknowledge those who have courageously given of themselves in leadership.

7. We see religion, magick and wisdom-in-living as being united in the way one views the world and lives within it—a world view and philosophy of life which we identify as *Witchcraft, the Wiccan Way.*

8. Calling oneself "Witch" does not make a Witch—but neither does heredity itself, nor the collecting of titles, degrees and initiations. A Witch seeks to control the forces within her/himself that make life possible in order to live wisely and well without harm to others and in harmony with Nature.

9. We believe in the affirmation and fulfillment of life in a continuation of evolution and development of consciousness, that gives meaning to the Universe we know, and our personal role within it.

10. Our only animosity towards Christianity, or toward any other religion or philosophy of life, is to the extent that its

institutions have claimed to be "the only way" and have sought to deny freedom to others and to suppress other ways of religious practice and belief.

11. American Witches, we are not threatened by debates on the history of the craft, the origins of various terms, the origins of various aspects of different traditions. We are concerned with our present and our future.

12. We do not accept the concept of absolute evil, nor do we worship any entity known as "Satan" or "the Devil," as defined by Christian tradition. We do not seek power through the suffering of others, nor do we accept that personal benefit can be derived only by denial to another.

13. We believe that we should seek within Nature that which is contributory to our health and well-being.

In October 2021, *USA Today* ran a story about modern witches with the quote: "No longer considered wicked, witches are hip." But that "in more recent times, those who have publicly identified as being witches said they faced discrimination and harassment. The numbers of Americans who identify with Wicca or paganism has risen from 134,000 in 2001 to nearly 2 million today, according to Helen Berger, a resident scholar at Brandeis University's Women's Studies Research Center, who has conducted extensive research and authored four books about witches and pagans."

The hashtag #whatwitcheslooklike trended worldwide leading up to Halloween 2021, with people from all walks of life, male and female, posting selfies demonstrating how normal witches can look, in opposition to the old stereotypes of the appearances of witches. On the hashtag's Instagram feed, a headline from a 2018 *Newsweek* article was included: "Number of Witches Rises Dramatically Across U.S. As Millennials Reject Christianity."

The Maetreum of Cybele on Route 23A in Pallenville sits on three acres of land at the foot of the famous Kaaterskill Clove and is "a reclaiming of the ancient Mother Goddess tradition updated to reflect modern times." The Reverend Cathryn Platine is the principal founder of the Cybeline Revival, which held its first public ritual back on March 24, 1999, and with the Maetreum has "re-introduced to the world a model for Pagan Monasticism." New Moon, Full Moon, and other rituals are held there, with the public invited to join in.

In personal correspondence with me, Cathryn wanted all to be aware that "we won a major decision on the equal protection of minority religions regarding zoning and property taxation, and it is important to note we own and operate the first Pagan owned FM radio station in the country, WLPP-LP." On November 18, 2014, the New York Court of Appeals handed down a decision that fully recognizes the religious nature of the Maetreum's property. "The last Pagan Emperor of Rome and devotee of Cybele, Julian, charged Pagans to 'Be thou the one,' referring to doing public works and charity and thus providing a living example to the rest of the world. We live by this at the Maetreum. We challenge other Pagans to follow our example and be thou the one by coming out of their broom closets and being open and active members of their local communities," Reverend Cathryn stated. The coffee/tea cafe, Bell Book and Candle, has open-house hours every Saturday between 1:00 and 4:00 p.m., and every Sunday at 5:00 p.m. training sessions are held for anybody interested in becoming more involved with the religious community there. Among planned events for the coming year are a Pagan Pride Day and the All Women's Festival.

The Church of Knotted Ash in upstate New York exists to "assist fellow Pagans in their communion with the gods through various levels of instruction ranging from general reverence of divinity to serious clergy training." It is home to the Coven of the Albino Bat, Tonawanda; Coven of the White Wolf, North Tonawanda; and Coven of the Grey Lynx, Albany. The church holds an annual retreat each summer in addition to a ten-week Wicca 101 course at their western New York location on Thursday nights, which covers, among other topics, ethics, etiquette, and elemental correspondences.

In August 2017 Susan Harris wrote an article titled "New York State: America's Witchcraft Capital" where she mentions that Westchester's News 12 reporter Tara Rosenblum spent four months interviewing local Hudson Valley practitioners of Wicca and witchcraft. Tara's journalism career is something to be admired; she is one of the most award-winning reporters in the state of New York, with more than 200 industry awards including a 2017 National Edward R. Murrow Award, 25 Emmy wins, and 105 Emmy nominations, and has twelve days named in her honor in communities across New York.

Tara's two-part video story *Speak No Evil* first aired August 29, 2017, and featured some Hudson Valley direct descendants of British witches that were executed. According to one witch interviewed, modern-day Hudson Valley sits on top of quartz crystal, with that energy being used and harnessed in ritual.

Some individuals interviewed by Tara were keeping their practices and beliefs secret in order to protect their careers, feeling that they would be less respected in the workplace. According to News 12, "Third-degree Wiccan high priestess Lisa Stewart said the duotheistic religion is a mysterious, feminist and nature-focused religion that rewards faith and patience with magic. They said their magic is capable of things like curing illnesses, getting a raise at work and helping people find love. Wiccans adhere to a strict moral code similar to the concept of karma. They believe that whatever your action is, good or evil, it will come back to you threefold. Stewart and her husband run the only legally recognized Wiccan church in the state. The Church of the Eternal Circle is housed right behind their metaphysical shop in New Paltz. Customers can have their spirits cleansed, spells cast or long-lost loved ones summoned."

In the 1970s when asked why there was a growth in magical groups, anthropologist Edward Moody explained that it is "an attempt by various people to regain a sense of control over their environment and their lives." This appears to be true in today's world as well. The concept of control over one's environment is one of the reasons why New York City's oldest witchcraft store, Enchantments, is never affected by economic downturns, recession, or pandemic. Enchantments opened its doors in 1982 to provide supplies to practitioners as well as guidance. They will not do spells such as love spells—anything they deem to be tampering with one's free will.

Witch Artifacts

We are fortunate to have had historians, restorers, and professors in New York State devote their life to documenting their finds on the subject of witchcraft. This region is rich with folklore and historical artifacts. In the hustle and bustle of modern life, it's interesting to look back at how seemingly primitive our immigrant ancestors lived.

Darrell Pinckney, of the Caretakers of History project, wrote in personal correspondence to me that witch bottles were used for rituals as early as the late sixteenth to early seventeenth century and that they were based on earlier rituals of the Netherlands and Germany. Bottles were buried under the foundation of a house in order to bind a guardian spirit to the area and actively protect the structure.

The belief evolved over time where the bottle would trap the evil spirits and influences, thus protecting the house in a more passive manner. A variant of this practice included trapping the evil spirits in the bottle and then throwing it into water, where they would be destroyed.

In seventeenth- and eighteenth-century Britain, the "cursed" put their toenails and fingernails, urine, and hair into the witch bottles. These jugs were usually buried near a house or building, where they were meant to keep evildoers at bay.

Notes on Witch Bottles

One type of witch bottle is stamped with the face of a bearded, grimacing man, possibly the anti-Protestant cardinal and inquisitor Roberto Bellarmine (1542–1621). Known as Bellarmines, or "Greybeards," these bottles were made of brown or gray stoneware glazed with salt. Bellarmine witch bottles have not been identified prior to 1650 or post-1700. Later witch bottles were made from glass bottles, small glass vials, and a variety of other containers.

Since at least the early modern period it has been a common custom to hide objects such as written charms, dried cats, horse skulls, concealed shoes, and witch bottles in the structure of a building. Some believe that witch bottles protect against evil spirits and magical attack, and counteract spells cast by witches. Witch bottles are countermagical devices, the purpose of which is to *draw in* and *trap* harmful intentions directed at their owners. Historically, the witch bottle contained the victim's urine, hair or nail clippings, or red thread. In recent times, the witch bottle is filled with rosemary, needles and pins, and red wine.

The bottle is then buried at the farthest corner of the property or beneath the house hearth, or placed in an inconspicuous spot in the house. It is believed that after being buried, the bottle captures evil, which is impaled on the pins and needles, drowned by the wine, and sent away by the rosemary. Some witch bottles were thrown into a fire and when they exploded, the spell was broken or the witch supposedly killed.

"Pins and nails" symbolizes the victim's pain. Boiling serves to redirect pain back to the witch. The inverted position of the bottle symbolizes the reversing or overturning of the witch's intentions.

On October 31, 2019, the *New Yorker* featured an article written by Geoff Manaugh on the topic of witch bottles and witch houses in New York State, explaining that "concealed objects are nearly always found close to openings and portals: doors, windows, and, in particular, chimneys—a chimney, [Brian] Hoggard told me, being an unnervingly open 'passageway from the sky.' [Walter] Wheeler's database shows that objects were hidden in similar places in Hudson Valley homes." "It's pretty clear," Hoggard was quoted in the article as saying, "that people believed magic could come into their homes through those points and that they were trying to thwart it."

Walter Wheeler, of Hartgen Archeological Associates, and fellow contractors discovered remnants throughout New York State of witch houses and witch bottles. Hartgen, with offices in New York and Vermont, is known as "the Northeast's leader in Cultural Resource Management" since 1973 and has recorded over five thousand successfully completed cultural resource studies.

Artifacts were found during renovations stuffed away in various locations. Sigils (symbols) carved by ancient hands were also discovered: "runes, astrological diagrams, alchemical signs," as Walter described to me in a telephone conversation.

Fortunately for us all, Walter recognized these finds as historical and significant and worthy of preservation. He began interviewing his elderly colleagues before it was too late, before the artifacts and their clues would be lost to time.

The Verplanck House, Beacon, Dutchess County, New York. Library of Congress

Binding and banishing artifacts were found in some of New York State's oldest houses. Some dated back to the 1600s, and were meant as protection against evil or bad magic.

Coeymans-Bronck House, State Route 144, Coeymans, Albany County, New York. Library of Congress

According to Geoff Manaugh's article in the *New Yorker*, "The spells of witches and other malevolent beings could be deflected to target a witch bottle, rather than a person, by the human elements stored within it (urine, fingernails, and hair); once the evil spirit was inside the bottle, the bent nails and pins, given new life on the other side, would wound or kill it. . . . Wheeler and Hoggard have found that, in both Britain and the Hudson Valley, children's shoes were often packed into peripheral voids around a house—the artifacts may also have been intended as targets for witches, in lieu of a home's living residents. Such voids could also contain 'curse dolls,' miniature human forms intended to stand in for the objects of spells."

In his personal correspondence to me, Darrell Pinckney also described items as being "apotropaic," meaning "something that has a power to avert or thwart bad luck or evil intent by another. In many ways, those items could also be called *amulets*."

Darrell continued: "Items like those described are also difficult to find. The belief in witchcraft was not as prevalent in the US as much as other nations, especially as the Great Awakening was occurring in the American colonies during the 18th century. This does not mean that it didn't occur. Some items were kept concealed in the walls of buildings. When items like these are encountered, it is often during an archaeological investigation conducted on a property deemed historically sensitive by SHPO [State Historic Preservation Office] or the township, or may be eligible for registration in the National Register of Historic Places. Therefore, I'm sure there are properties that were altered, modified, etc., that may have contained similar items that we never hear about, especially if the property or structures on it are torn down, removed, modified, etc. Some of the items may not even be recognized by property owners or contractors who are modifying properties with older existing structures. They become reburied or discarded during the construction phases."

But other theories on these artifacts include the school of thought that witch bottles were meant to be medicinal in nature and protect the home's occupant in that regard.

One of the houses studied and visited by Geoff Manaugh for his *New Yorker* article is the Albertus Van Loon House in Athens, and he describes how entering the house felt like traveling through a portal back to earlier times. It is one of the oldest known homes in New York State, and its current owners shared their many finds, including children's shoes, quartz pieces, and a decapitated doll.

Located at 85 North Washington Street, the house was built by one of Jan Van Loon's eight sons, with Jan being the first known European settler to the Athens area, originally called Loonenburg. The house was occupied by three generations of the Van Loon family after Albertus passed, ending the family ownership of the house in the early twentieth century.

From Walter Wheeler's findings:

Protective rituals and practices associated with undertaking building and occupation of dwellings and public buildings were brought to North America by early European immigrants. There they met aboriginal magical practices, and were transformed over time. Talismanic rituals included scribing symbolic markings or carvings on the building (particularly at entrances and stairways), foundation deposits (coins, quartz crystals, cornerstone deposits), and site-specific deposits such as broken ceramics placed under hearth stones, shoes placed in walls or floors, horse shoes over doors, and horse skulls at eaves, etc., and topping out ceremonies. These practices were actively engaged in until the middle decades of the 19th century; some survive today.

Evidence for these practices has been found at early 17th century archeological sites in Albany, New York, and elsewhere in the Hudson Valley of New York and New Jersey, and can be traced through archeological sites and standing structures throughout the New World Dutch cultural hearth.

Irish, British, and Dutch immigrants brought their belief in magic with them. "Some evidence points to the possibility of the appeasement of local gods in claiming a place for a home, and the sanctification of the home as a place for dwelling," Wheeler stated in his findings. "The region identified was originally occupied by several different tribes of Native Americans, including the Algonquian Lenape, Mohawks and Mahicans. Settlement in the region by people of European extraction began in 1614 with the establishment of a trading post near today's Albany, New York, and at about the same time on Manhattan Island. Although the initial European settlers in this region originated from many different countries, the largest number were Dutch and the largest tracts of land were purchased or controlled by families from that country."

Not only just of local interest, Walter's work was then shared at conferences in England and Luxembourg. In England, Walter presented his findings at Hidden Charms, a biannual conference put together by Brian Hoggard, a British historian and musician, whose work on the topic is also fascinating. Brian's book *Magical House Protection: The Archaeology of Counter-Witchcraft* concentrates on mostly Britain and his folklore findings from the mid-fourteenth century to the present.

Since Walter and I are practically neighbors, I reached out to him and we spoke on the telephone about his belief that artifacts will continue to be found while renovating historic homes in New York State.

He told me of his appearance on the History Channel's *The UnXplained* with William Shatner in 2020 for the episode "Mysterious Curses" where he and Brian Hoggard explained the belief in protecting openings such as fireplaces, windows, and doors from evil entering a home—beliefs brought here from England and Germany, for example. I had seen the episode prior to knowing him and was pleased to watch it again having been able to speak with him.

Throughout North America and England, shoes were the most common worn objects found hidden away in old homes. Walter listed many New York homes where shoes were found tucked away in various locations. These include the Verplanck house/Beacon, Gayhead Hamlet/East Fishkill, Smit house/New Paltz, Gomez house/Newburgh, Philip Deyo house/New Paltz, Cunning house/Galway, Gamage house/Saratoga, Sanders house/Charlton, Philip Schuyler house/Schuylerville, Van Alen house/DeFreestville, Schoolcraft house/Guilderland, Coeymans-Bronck house/Coeymans, Graham-Brush house/Pine Plains, Ebenezer Jarvis house/Huntington, O. Button house/Canajoharie, Latting's Hundred/Huntington, Cooper-Mann house/Sussex Borough,

Johnson Hall/Johnstown, Clapp house/Pittstown, and Peter Vrooman house/Schoharie.

General Philip Schuyler House, Schuylerville, New York, vintage postcard.
Author's Collection

In 1958 many shoes (some as old as the 1700s) were found tucked away in the General Philip Schuyler House in Schuylerville. Schuyler was third in command after George Washington. The estate is part of the 1684 Saratoga Patent of 168,000 acres granted to seven New Yorkers, and the house itself has a rich history and turmoil from before and after the battles of Saratoga. During a raid by Indians and Canadians in 1745, the farm and estate were largely wiped out. The original house was burned by the British and rebuilt during a cold fall of 1777.

A recent site curator in communication with Walter revealed that among the artifacts that mark this important home's history are: "behind stairs in kitchen wing; c. 1860s rubber overshoe marked 'Priscilla Stover' found in a wall; additional shoes found in walls including a c. 1790 woman's slipper." With the tumultuous history of the house and property, it's no wonder that its inhabitants would incorporate the use of protection talismans.

In New Paltz, similar objects were found in the Philip and Gertrude Deyo house. According to the Town of New Paltz Landmark Nomination Form, "An oft-repeated story about a nail shortage during the Revolutionary War prompting Philip Deyo to go to Kingston to collect nails after the British burned the town in 1777 is the principal reference." The house is significant due to its being one of the original eighteen stone houses remaining from the 1700s in New Paltz.

In his research, Walter Wheeler shared:

A small child's shoe, bearing signs of wear, was discovered in an internal wall of the Van Alen house, in DeFreestville, NY. The house was constructed in 1793 for John E. and Anne Freyenmoet van Alen, who were childless. After the completion of the house their nephew Evert moved in with them, but the couple never had any children of their own. The couple was practicably past child-bearing age, and so it is unlikely that the intention was to invoke fertility, and the shoe did not come from a member of the immediate family. It is possible that one of [the] family's 10 slaves provided the shoe; alternatively, it may have been contributed by one of the builders. In either case, a more complex intention is suggested by this example. Popular thinking on the subject assigns magical value to all articles of clothing, "from their intimate association with [a] . . . person." This notion is extended to the belief that even footprints cut from the earth have magical potential.

According to Walter's research, some of the more dramatic artifacts found in the region's houses include the following:

A human skull was found during the course of renovation work at the Coeymans house in Coeymans, NY, in 2008. This artifact had initially been recovered in 1971, but had been redeposited in the sealed alcove provided for it in the foundation wall, and subsequently was forgotten. Staff at the New York State Museum have conducted tests on the skull, and have determined it to have belonged to a woman who lived during the 18th century, who died between the ages of 30 and 50, and who was scalped shortly before her death. The foundation that the skull was found within dates to c. 1720.

Along the same lines as Darrell Pinckney's research on witch bottles, Walter's findings include:

Turpentine or other strong-smelling liquid, was found in the second floor of the south gable end wall of the c. 1750 Rysedorph house in North Greenbush, NY, when the house was undergoing renovations in 1978. The bottle dates to the early 19th century. Its contents have not been fully examined. A sealed clear glass bottle believed to date to the early 19th century and containing fingernail clippings was found in an area at the southern portion of the Schuyler Flatts in the Town of Colonie, NY, between 1971 and 1974. The context in which the bottle was found was not associated with a construction episode, but was however, in close proximity to much earlier burials. The folklore of nearby Schoharie County attributes magical powers to fingernail clippings, including the ability to attract a love interest, and protection against rheumatism. This belief is related to English folklore, which in recorded examples dating to as late as 1939 identify nail clippings as principal components of witch bottles. Glass bottles, apparently empty of contents but with interior staining, are not infrequently found in the vicinity of the Mohawk Valley. They are typically found in inaccessible parts of the structure of wood-framed houses and are believed to have contained urine, but none have been tested. Local lore indicates that when constructing a new house one should place such a bottle in the framing "for luck" or in defense against witches. One such example was found in the Houck house (c. 1805), Town of Florida (Montgomery County), NY, in the north wall of a second floor bed chamber.

Here in New York State, Native Americans were the first to equate quartz crystals with protecting powers, believing these crystals to signify light and well being, and also used them to sanctify living spaces. A seventeenth-century Native American trader's house near Albany had such crystals placed in corners of the dwelling.

Slaves from East and West Africa and Madagascar were brought to New York by 1625, and from Manhattan Island to Albany. Their belief system incorporated usage of bundles containing shells, crystals, pins, and broken pottery, which were believed to house spirits. These bundles, which have been found in buildings in New York that they were known to have occupied, may have been used as protection and in conjuring rituals or in divination and predicting the future, then buried in confined spaces within a dwelling.

Today a private residence, but from 1739 until the farming ceased in the 1950s, Latting's Hundred in Huntington, Long Island, also served as a general store, post office, and inn, with many generations of African Americans living and working there alongside the residence's family during that time period. One such bundle described above was found buried in a cellar stairway. Walter Wheeler's findings on this ancient house originally built in 1653 mention: "a cache of artifacts which according to the discoverer, 'consists of 2 bent wrought iron nails with simple curve, 2 bent wrought iron nails with compound curve, 2 matched brass waistcoat buttons, 1 flat bone disc button, 1 glass Indian Trade seed bead with red exterior over white core, 2 bent brass hand-headed pins, 1 small scallop shell, 1 upholstery tack with brass head and iron shank, 1 small sliver of rawhide, 2 shards of green bottle glass, 2 shards of salt glazed stoneware with cobalt blue spirals over a white clay body and 1 quartz crystal spearhead with a broken tip

(Native American Archaic Period). They were placed together, on top of a twisted cellar beam, between the beam and the floorboards and were contained or held in place with a rolled piece of sheer linen, about 18 inches long.' (Fig. 12) The bundle was found under the top of a stair leading to a basement room occupied by one of the family's slaves." The Native American Archaic period referenced in the quote lasted from around 8000 BC to 1000 BC, and these types of spearheads were used before the invention of the bow and arrow.

"A third assemblage," Walter continues, "consisting of two necklaces made of blue and white glass Indian trade beads was found in the cellar of the main house, on top of an exposed portion of the northwest end sill, behind the parlor chimney stack. The colors and placement of these necklaces on the northwest wall of the house are thought to have apotropaic connotations."

In 1972, according to Water, "a Brazilian 10 réis coin bearing the date 1736, and drilled twice for wearing as a pendant, was uncovered in excavations on State Street—the principal street of Albany in the 18th century. The coin features an 'X' prominently on one of its faces; it has been speculated that this may be another example of the use of this device, as a personal charm, in this case."

Like evergreens, horseshoes were believed to be effective protections near entrances since witches could not come under a horseshoe.

Marriages between Native Americans, slaves, and white immigrants were inevitable, resulting in the sharing of belief systems and symbols such as the white and blue beads, corn cobs, and moccasins that were tucked away within old houses from the

1700s from Manhattan to Albany. Items excavated from burial sites in Manhattan have led some scholars to believe that these items were important rites of passage in the individual's journey to adulthood or the afterlife.

From Joseph Glanvill's *Saducismus Triumphatus,* or *Evidence concerning Witches and Apparitions* (1681) comes this: "He advised him to take a Bottle, and put his Wife's Urine into it, together with Pins and Needles and Nails, and Cork them up, and set the Bottle to the fire. The Man followed the prescription . . . but at last . . . the Cork bounced out, and the Urine, Pins, Nails and Needles all flew up . . . and his Wife continued in the same trouble and languishment still. Not long after, the Old Man came to the house again, and inquired . . . how his Wife did . . . Ha, quoth he . . . now I will put you in a way that will make the business sure. Take your Wife's Urine as before, and cork it in a Bottle with Nails, Pins and Needles, and bury it in the Earth. The Man did accordingly. And his Wife began to mend . . . and in a competent time was finely well recovered. But there came a Woman from a Town some miles off to their house, with a lamentable Out-cry, that they had killed her Husband . . . that . . . Husband was a Wizzard and had bewitched this Mans Wife. Some hair, the parings of the nails, and urine, of any person bewitched . . . being put into a stone bottle with crooked nails, corked closed, and tied down with wire, and hung up the chimney, will cause the Witch to suffer the most acute torments imaginable, till the bottle is uncorked, and the mixture dispersed; insomuch that they will even risk a detection, by coming to the house, and attempting to pull down the bottle."

It's been said that curses only have power if you believe in them.

In the 2017 *Practical Magic* issue of *Faire Magazine*, Veronica Varlow's Woodstock Magic House was featured and beautifully photographed as well. It was a hundred-year-old cottage she was restoring until it completely burned in 2011, to be rebuilt and restored again, with the new house called Curiosa Magic House. The house was purposely aligned with the four cardinal directions. Veronica placed in the wet cement for the foundation blessed botanicals: rosebuds for love, mugwort for dreams and creativity, linden flowers for sweetness in the home, allspice for abundance, thistle for protection, and orange peels for joy. In the fireplace mortar to hold the bricks, she placed these same blessed botanicals plus cinnamon and rosemary. "The bones of Magic House, each board of wood underneath the drywall, has spells, sigils, and incantations written on it," Veronica stated.

"On the second level," Veronica said, "a jute rope stretches across the cascading wall of windows that draws the moonlight and the sweet sunbeams in. Upon that rope, I hung three white dresses to lure the muses of magic and creativity in, pretty things for them to wear when they arrive. The center dress is a cream Victorian lace dress that I wore in a ritual with sixteen other witches in the river that runs below Magic House, when we performed a midsummer self-marriage ceremony. The hundred-year-old cream lace is tattered from that gorgeous day as I hiked through the woods with my sisters of the Magic House Coven to the river. The lace still holds some of the pieces of twigs and leaves from the forest." The house is stunningly unique, with windows placed to allow for maximum moonlight and sunlight to enter. She also shared that her Grandma Helen loved to use the sound of bells to clear the air and move stuck energy in a home.

Since 2015 Veronica has been holding Love Witch retreats four times a year here, with all the tuition from the retreats going back into the house. Witch Camp was started there, with visitors from around the world attending. In the *Practical Magic* issue referenced above, Veronica outlines steps to create your own magic house.

Cornell's Witchcraft Collection

New York is where the first, oldest known written book on the subject of witchcraft is permanently housed. The *Fortalicium Fidei* dates from 1497 and was previously owned by a monastery of St. Maximin at Trèves. It now resides at the Cornell University Library, having been acquired by George Lincoln Burr on one of his many European book-buying trips.

According to Cornell University's Digital Collection, where there also resides a pen-and-ink drawing of Burr, "George Lincoln Burr, Cornell Class of 1877, was Cornell University President Andrew D. White's personal secretary and librarian. Originally hired when he was a sophomore, Burr worked closely and collaboratively with President White in collecting the over 30,000 books that White donated to the Cornell University Library."

And according to Rossell Hope Robbins, "the biggest and best collection in the world to study witchcraft" is also at Cornell. His book *The Encyclopedia of Witchcraft and Demonology*, originally published in 1959, presents the knowledge and findings of Andrew White and George Burr. Some original source material can be found in the Reserve Room of the New York Public Library.

On Halloween 2017, Cornell University held the opening of the largest exhibit of witchcraft in North America, *The World Bewitch'd: Visions of Witchcraft from the Cornell Collections*. Held in the Kroch Library, it demonstrated the perception of women in society throughout history's witchcraft craze.

According to Cornell's website description of the event, "'The World Bewitch'd' is an exhibition exploring the origins and spread of the belief in witchcraft across Europe. Featuring rare and unique books and documents—from 15th-century witch hunting manuals to 20th-century movie posters—the exhibition examines themes such as gendered stereotypes, belief in night flying, shapeshifting, demonic pacts, and the witch epidemics that resulted in the deaths of tens of thousands. The World Bewitch'd offers a rare glimpse of the treasures of the Cornell Witchcraft Collection, established by Cornell University's first president, Andrew Dickson White, and now the largest in North America with more than 3,000 items."

The collection is noteworthy for its rare trial transcripts not available anywhere else and its holdings of trial records, including original manuscript depositions taken from victims in courthouses or torture chambers. The exhibit's online counterpart notes that even midwives were targeted as witches, because they were "likely to possess knowledge that could prevent conception, cause miscarriage, or sicken infants." And before the Middle Ages, men were most likely to be thought of as practitioners of the occult— men who were known to be "requiring skills and knowledge such as advanced scientific understanding, manipulation of magic, the commanding of demons, or negotiating pacts with the Devil. These men studied astrology, devised symbolic languages, and practiced divination." During the Middle Ages, due to the rise in book and pamphlet publication, witchcraft mania took hold in person and through the printed word with startling imagery.

Cornell University reiterates what has been documented many times through the centuries—that the definition of what constituted a witch was murky. Oftentimes it was simply superstitious perceptions of those in the community who were just different, or those who had quarrels with neighbors being targeted. Exhibition curators Anne Kenney and Kornelia Tancheva wanted to show the contrast between what witch hunting was versus the modern-day misuse of the term bandied about today.

Anne Sauer, director of Rare and Manuscript Collections, stated that Cornell's collection continues to grow, with a popular culture portion added in 2012 as well. Fortunately, you can view the exhibit online.

Katherine Howe, author of *The Penguin Book of Witches* (2014), sums up the fascination with witches this way: "There's a macabre interest to it. It's eerie and creepy and a little bit scary."

Today in America as well as in other countries, petitions are being circulated to pardon witches who were condemned and killed. These are long overdue to exonerate the poor souls who suffered and had their names blackened for all eternity.

Robert Poole, a professor of history at the University of Central Lancashire, speaking with *ITV Granada Reports*: "They [witches] were poor people, mostly women, on the margin of their communities. . . . They made a living by begging and casting spells on their neighbors' behalf, but when things went wrong those neighbors turned on them and gave evidence against them." He felt that this sort of petition was important in today's world to refrain from labeling community members as different to help prevent various miscarriages of justice from continuing to happen.

Friend, colleague, and fellow author Jennifer Billock, who also publishes the monthly subscription newsletter *KitchenWitch*, writes, "The push to maintain Catholic orthodoxy butted up against the strong sense of mountain folklore. The result? Increased fear of the witches."

"In 1994 the pope called for the Roman Catholic Church to 'examine its historical conscience.' One result is the formation of a Catholic commission in the Czech Republic—the first of its kind—to consider whether to pardon hundreds of people who were burned alive as witches," reported *The Watchtower*. The *Sunday Telegraph of London* reports, "The church may contemplate posthumous apologies." An Alabama coalition, Pagans in Action: Council for Truth, "asked the pope to apologize specifically for injustices suffered by their spiritual ancestors." The petition was signed by 1,641 neo-pagans, scholars, Christian clergy, neo-pagan organizations, and others; it was dated 1999-Samhain (October 31). The coalition describes neo-paganism as "a global spiritual movement that draws its inspiration and traditions from indigenous pre-Christian religions" according to EWTN News, and these attacks included forcing pagans to convert, desecrating their sacred sites, and collaborating with states to persecute and execute pagans during the Inquisition, which began during the thirteenth century. This group feels that the "Memory and Reconciliation" report by the Catholic Church and its vague apology doesn't address pagans directly and the injustices done to them.

All across the world, it is felt that it is now time for witches to rest in peace.

Witch is not to be a misogynist slur anymore, but rather a witch is an empowered person in command of their environment.

Bad or beautiful, witches will always fascinate us.

Bibliography

Arkins, Diane C. *Halloween: Romantic Art and Customs of Yesteryear*. Gretna, LA: Pelican Publishing, 2000.

Bannatyne, Lesley Pratt. *Halloween: An American Holiday, An American History*. New York: Facts on File, 1990.

Bannatyne, Lesley Pratt. *Halloween Nation: Behind the Scenes of America's Fright Night*. Gretna, LA: Pelican Publishing, 2011.

Bell, Blake A. "Ralph and Mary Hall (Persecuted in the 17th Century for Witchcraft) Fled to the Manor of Pelham." *Pelham Weekly* 15, no. 34 (September 1, 2006): 8.

Billock, Jennifer. "Visit the Site of the Biggest Witch Trial in History." *Smithsonian Magazine*, September 14, 2016. https://www.smithsonianmag.com/travel/visit-site-biggest-witch-trial-history-180959946.

Burr, George Lincoln, ed. *Narratives of the Witchcraft Cases 1648–1706*. New York: C. Scribner's Sons, 1914.

Burr, George Lincoln, ed. "Witchcraft in New York: The Cases of Hall and Harrison." From *Narratives of the Witchcraft Cases 1648–1706* (New York: C. Scribner's Sons, 1914). Accessed from Hanover Historical Texts Project, Hanover College, https://history.hanover.edu/texts/nyhah.html.

Byrne, John Aiden. "BOO York: Big Apple Is No. 1 City for Witches." *New York Post*, October 30, 2021. https://nypost .com/2021/10/30/the-big-apple-has-been-named-the-best-city -for-witches.

Caro, Tina. "Is Witchcraft Illegal in New York?" Magickal Spot. https://magickalspot.com/is-witchcraft-illegal-in-new-york.

Cornell University. "The World Bewitch'd: Visions of Witchcraft from the Cornell Collections." https://rmc.library.cornell.edu/ witchcraft.

Cresswell, Joanna. "Intimate Photos of Modern-Day Witches across America." CNN in partnership with Refinery29, November 28, 2018. https://www.cnn.com/style/article/witches-in-america -frances-f-denny-refinery-29/index.html.

Dawson, Mackenzie. "Sleepy Hollow Has More to Offer Than a Headless Horseman." *New York Post*, October 4, 2013. https:// nypost.com/2013/10/04/sleepy-hollow-has-more-to-offer -than-a-headless-horseman.

Drake, Samuel Gardner. *Annals of Witchcraft*. Boston: W. Elliot Woodward, 1869.

EWTN News. "Pagans Call for Apology from Catholics." February 11, 2000. http://www.ewtn.com.

Haefeli, Evan. "Dutch New York and the Salem Witch Trials: Some New Evidence." Proceedings of the American Antiquarian Society, 2003. https://www.americanantiquarian .org/proceedings/44539518.pdf.

Henderson, John R. "The Witch of Salem, New York." ICYouSee. Last modified January 29, 2014. www.icyousee.org/witch.html.

Hoffman, Alice. *Practical Magic*. New York: Berkley/Penguin Random House, 1995.

Hoffman, Alice. *The Rules of Magic*. New York: Simon and Schuster, 2017.

Howe, Katherine, ed. *The Penguin Book of Witches*. New York: Penguin Classics, 2014.

Irving, Washington. *The Legend of Sleepy Hollow and Other Stories*. New York: Penguin Classics, 2014.

Kelley, Ruth E. *The Book of Hallowe'en*. Boston: Lothrop, Lee & Shepard Co., 1919.

Kruk, Jonathan. *Legends and Lore of Sleepy Hollow and the Hudson Valley*. Charleston, SC: History Press, 2011.

Levermore, Charles H. "Witchcraft in Connecticut." *New Englander* 44 (1885): 788–817.

Levin, Ira. *Rosemary's Baby*. New York: Pegasus Books, 2017.

Manaugh, Geoff. "Witch Houses of the Hudson Valley." *New Yorker*, October 31, 2019. https://www.newyorker.com/culture/culture-desk/witch-houses-of-the-hudson-valley.

McMurry, James. *The Catskill Witch*. Syracuse, NY: Syracuse University Press, 1974.

Mueller, Mickie. *Llewellyn's Little Book of Halloween*. Woodbury, MN: Llewellyn Publications, 2018.

Mufuzi, Friday. "The Practice of Witchcraft and the Changing Patterns of Its Paraphernalia in the Light of Technologically Produced Goods as Presented by Livingstone Museum, 1930s–1973." *Zambia Social Science Journal* 5, no. 1 (2017). https://scholarship.law.cornell.edu/zssj/vol5/iss1/5.

News 12 Staff. "Speak No Evil: Wiccan Witchcraft Growing in Hudson Valley." News 12 Westchester, August 29, 2017. https://westchester.news12.com/speak-no-evil-wiccan-witchcraft-growing-in-hudson-valley-36244941.

Paull, Marion. *Creating Your Vintage Halloween*. London: CICO Books, 2014.

Rajchel, Diana. *Mabon: Rituals, Recipes & Lore for the Autumn Equinox*. Woodbury, MN: Llewellyn Publications, 2015.

Rajchel, Diana. *Samhain: Rituals, Recipes & Lore for Halloween*. Woodbury, MN: Llewellyn Publications, 2015.

RavenWolf, Silver. *Solitary Witch*. Woodbury, MN: Llewellyn Publications, 2003.

"Revolutionary War Cemetery." Town of Salem, New York. https://salem-ny.com/revolutionary-war-cemetery.

Sciortino, Dina. "Hulda, the Witch That Put a Spell on Sleepy Hollow, Healed Her Neighbors and Fought in the Revolutionary War." *Westchester Woman*, September 25, 2015. http://westchesterwoman.org/haunted-westchester-meet-hulda-the-witch-that-put-a-spell-on-sleepy-hollow-healed-her-neighbors-and-fought-in-the-revolutionary-war.

Shakespeare, William. *Mr. William Shakespeare's Comedies, Histories, & Tragedies: Published According to the True Original Copies*. London, 1623.

Snider, Amber C. "The Enchanting Witches of New York." Culture Trip, June 28, 2019. https://theculturetrip.com/north-america/usa/new-york/new-york-city/articles/the-enchanting-witches-of-new-york.

Time Traveler's Genealogy Page. "Witchcraft Trials in New York (1665)." Rootsweb, updated July 9, 2000. http://homepages.rootsweb.com/~tmetrvlr/hd10.html.

Wikipedia. "Katherine Harrison." Last modified May 4, 2021. https://en.wikipedia.org/wiki/Katherine_Harrison.

Wikipedia. Thirteen Principles of Belief, from "American Council of Witches." Last modified December 24, 2021. https://en.wikipedia.org/wiki/American_Council_of_Witches.

Williams, Marie. "Westchester County's Katharine Harrison, Accused Witch." *New York Almanack*, October 29, 2919. https://newyorkhistoryblog.org/2019/10/westchester-countys-katharine-harrison-accused-witch.

The Witch's Voice Inc. https://witchvox.com.

Acknowledgments

Many talented people helped me on this journey of writing a book on witchcraft and what I felt was important to New York State history—stories important to tell and gather in one place. Thank you to Peter Corina of Cornell University for lending such rich ancient illustrations. Thanks also go to James McMurry, author of *The Catskill Witch*, who wrote to me in 2013 giving me permission to include his stories in my books and said: "The Catskill Witch was my anchor in the past, securing me to our beloved Washington Irving. Look long at the Hudson River once for me." To Shelby Mattice of the Bronck Museum for giving me history on our Hudson Valley Region when I met her at a Hudson Fortnightly Club presentation. To Walter Wheeler for his research and artifact finding and for practically being my neighbor, with many phone calls to share his work with me. And to Caity Lail at the Hudson Staples for helping me so much over the years with my art projects; she is someone who goes over and above the scope of her job.

About the Author

Lisa LaMonica is an author and illustrator living in upstate New York, who has won numerous awards for her artwork. Her books include *Haunted Catskills* and *Images of America: Hudson*. She has written for such outlets as *Chronogram* magazine and PBS/WMHT.